GW00391057

The Bard in the Bush

John Fraser

The Bard in the Bush

Illustrations by Magnus Lohkamp

HART-DAVIS, MACGIBBON
GRANADA PUBLISHING
London Toronto Sydney New York

Published by Granada Publishing in
Hart-Davis, MacGibbon Ltd 1978

Granada Publishing Limited
Frogmore, St Albans, Herts AL2 2NF
and
3 Upper James Street, London W1R 4BP
1221 Avenue of the Americas, New York, NY 10020 USA
117 York Street, Sydney, NSW 2000, Australia
100 Skyway Avenue, Toronto, Ontario, Canada M9W 3A6
Trio City, Coventry Street, Johannesburg 2001, South Africa

ISBN 0 246 11014 7

Printed in Great Britain by
Butler & Tanner Ltd, Frome and London

For Sue,
without whom this book would not have
been possible, and who will have to
take part of the blame, as it is based
on both our diaries.

All the events in the following pages happened.

I have changed several names to avoid embarrassment or
legal action.

Acknowledgement

I should like to thank all those people who gave us so much help and hospitality, and particularly the British Council for financing and arranging our trip.

Above all, we are profoundly grateful to Valerie West for her unflagging assistance and enthusiasm, and for her trust in our talent and stamina.

Contents

Contents

Prologue

The British Council is a gigantic organisation dedicated to all sorts of good works and esoteric diplomatic wheelings and dealings of which I understand nothing. They have a magnificent headquarters in The Mall, all stainless steel and bronze, glass and whispering lifts that whisk you to the top floor before you have time to gulp. The Department of Music and Drama is not in this most prestigious of buildings. It is tucked away in a shabby annex in Davies Street, well out of range of the Household Cavalry and the clicking cameras. In Government circles, 'The Arts' would appear to be considered either embarrassing or unnecessary.

The Council employees in this backwater, however, are unabashed. They work like beavers, arranging for concerts and plays and ballet companies to be sent all over the world, often to the most inaccessible and unlikely places. It is partly cultural flag-waving, but to the audiences in those remote parts it must seem like philanthropy.

Being addicted to travel and exotic countries, and having made a reasonable living and a reputation of one sort or another as an actor, I offered them my services. I had in mind the dazzlingly original idea of a two-handed anthology type of programme based on Byron or The Class War or anything else they could suggest, preferably with songs thrown in as I can play six on my guitar. They were the very soul of politeness, but they allowed me to leave the office without a binding contract. 'Don't call us, we'll call you.' They did.

*

9

I was rehearsing for the last episode of a television serial which, though not beneath contempt as I was being paid for it, did not make impossible demands on my intelligence, and would make even less on that of the viewers. As several months had elapsed since my visit to Davies Street, I'd almost forgotten I'd ever been there as I suffer from the opposite of total recall. The assistant floor manager informed me that I was wanted on the 'phone.

'John? This is Julie from the British Council.'

'Hello Julie!'

'Would you be interested in going for two months to Sierra Leone, Nigeria and Cameroon?'

'When?'

'In three weeks.' Just when my serial ended.

'Yes!' Sierra Leone, Nigeria, Cameroon! My imagination took wing.

'That's splendid. There's practically no money, of course.'

'Of course.'

'But we pay your expenses.'

'I can play six songs on my guitar.'

'Well, I mean, that's up to you, but what they want is Shakespeare.'

'What play?'

'The tour has been arranged for school-children, and they've asked specifically for the plays they're studying. It'll help them with their exams.'

'Plays? You mean more than one? In three weeks?'

'If you can manage it, they'd like *Macbeth*, *The Merchant of Venice*, *The Taming of the Shrew*, *Henry V*, *Twelfth Night*, and perhaps *Julius Caesar* and *The Tempest* for Cameroon.'

'I see. Just *The Complete Works* in fact. Easy. Three weeks... Who's all going?'

'Only two of you.'

'Who's the other one?'

'We thought we'd better leave that to you.'

'Mm-hm. Who's directing?'

'You can put it together yourselves, can't you?'

'Oh, surely!' I felt as if I was swimming out of sight of land without a lifebelt. 'What were the plays again? *Hamlet, Othello, The Merchant of Venice...*'

Macbeth and *The Merchant* are the most popular, so if you concentrate on them, and just do *bits* from *Henry V, Julius Caesar, The Taming of the Shrew* – '

'I think I'd better come in and discuss this with you, Julie. I've never done anything like this before...'

'Of course. I'm so pleased you're interested.'

The rest of the rehearsal was a write-off. I fluffed my lines and banged into the furniture, my head whirling with the problems of compiling and adapting and casting and directing and fitting in snatches of 'Hang Down Your Head Tom Dooley'.

At our meeting, Julie and I agreed on three basic principles.

1. In the time at our disposal, we could not hope to prepare more than two plays in abridged versions. Perhaps we might consider preparing a third when we were 'on the road'.

2. Since *Macbeth* and *The Merchant* were the top favourites, my colleague should be female. (For *Henry V* or *Julius Caesar*, two males would have been necessary.)

3. There was no necessity, nor indeed any excuse, for including 'Tom Dooley'.

I had first to find an actress who would be prepared to accompany me on what Julie warned me would be a fairly arduous and sometimes uncomfortable trip. Someone, in fact, who could 'rough it', someone with whom I could 'get on' for two months inescapably in each other's constant company, and, not least, someone who could play Lady Macbeth and Portia.

Since playing opposite each other in one of the less distinguished and best forgotten *Doctor* films, Suzan Farmer and I had maintained a sporadic but affectionate friendship, based on a sympathetic understanding of the problems we seem to encounter in our respective love-lives, which I don't propose to go into here, and an inordinate capacity for bitter laughter. I knew she had the 'edge' for Lady Macbeth, and the grace for Portia, that in small doses at least she was an intelligent and witty companion, and that, quite simply, we should 'get on'. Furthermore, she has the kind of face and figure that one does not normally associate with 'British Cultural Flag-Waving', which I could not help feeling would be to our advantage.

My one nagging doubt was about her pioneering spirit. I had good reason to suspect it was absent. I have a summer house three thousand feet up a mountain in Tuscany, with no road, no electricity, and sometimes enough water for a weekly bidet-bath. I had invited her as a house-guest on more than one occasion, only to be jeered at and mocked for suggesting anything so insanitary. Her cottage in North London is all fitted carpets and Dresden figures and pale-velvet upholstery and banks of cabbage-roses round the door *with no green-fly*. Half her waking hours are spent in the bath or under the dryer. You just have to say 'spider' and she's over the horizon in a puff of dust.

I mustered all the tact and persuasion at my disposal, and rang her up. The line was engaged. It was engaged for half an hour. I could no longer contain all that mustered tact and persuasion, so I headed north and rang her bell.

Apart from the fact that Mrs Olive likes to do the housework in her bare feet, she is a remarkably unremarkable woman. She opened the door, gnarled tootsies peeking, and said, 'Yeah?' We have met on numerous occasions, but she resists any impulse to be effusive.

'Is Sue in, Mrs Olive?'

'She's sleepin'.' She closed the door and switched on the hoover. She took her time to answer my second ring, but when she did I got my foot in and kept it there.

'I'm sorry to be a nuisance, Mrs Olive, but it's really very important that I speak to Sue.'

'She's sleepin'.'

'Yes, so you said. But it's half-past eleven, and high time she was up.'

Her Neanderthal brow registered nothing of the inner conflict I was certain my persistence was causing her, though her toes were beating a tattoo on the mat. A light, unexpected shove, she was off balance, and I was in and up the stairs. From below I heard her shout something to the effect that I couldn't do what I had just undoubtedly done.

The bedroom was in darkness, though I could see that the telephone receiver was off the hook. I had to shout before the bed-clothes even stirred. It was not till much later that I was to discover the reason for this log-like repose. Sue sleeps with her good ear on the pillow. The other, or outward-pointing one, is purely for decoration, for it is as deaf as a meat-pie.

She sat bolt upright, clutching the sheet to her chin, her eyes bulging with alarm.

'Johnny! What's happened?'

'Sorry to wake you, love, but it's nearly lunchtime, and I've got something to ask – '

'What time is it?'

'Well...nearly twelve.'

'Oh God! I didn't get to bed till five. I've got a head like a lighthouse...'

'Hangover?'

'Well, I wasn't drinking tea after a first night, was I? I think I'm going to be sick. No – maybe I'm not.'

'Can I get you an Alka-Seltzer?'

'They're in the bathroom cupboard. What on earth are you doing here anyway?'

I fetched her the fizzing glass and let her quaff it.

'How would you like to play Lady Macbeth and Portia?'

'Where?'

I had hoped to win her over with the challenge of playing the two great roles before having to answer that one.

'The White Man's Grave.' I explained the whole project at length, emphasising that she may, on occasion, have to curb her passion for ablutions, that we would be travelling hundreds and hundreds of miles by Land Rover, that the audiences might be rowdy, food and accommodation poor, and that there were more lurgies on the Equator than were dreamt of in her philosophy.

After a long pause, all she said was, 'Oh, darling...', but I thought I detected a hint of excitement in her bleary eye. Then, 'What makes you think I can do it?' she asked.

'You're tough enough for Lady M., and you're classy enough and have the sense of fun for Portia. And if I can play Macbeth, Bassanio, *and* Shylock, you can do it all right. Even if we're terrible, they won't throw eggs in the jungle. At least I hope not. And Bernard Levin isn't going to be sitting in the front row.'

'I'll miss seeing my thriller.' She'd just finished a Racquel Welch type part in a play for A.T.V. which had yet to be seen.

'Not a good enough excuse. You can get Roy to tape it.'

'What a challenge. I haven't done Shakespeare since I left Central...'

'Well I've done lots. I'm going to be magnificent, so you'll have to come up with something or look silly.'

She leapt out of bed, threw open the curtains and the sun streamed in.

'I'll do it! I'll do it!' she squealed. 'I don't care about the lurgies! They have Flit don't they? Where's the Atlas?'

'And the *Complete Shakespeare!*'

And clutching those two titanic volumes, containing between their well-thumbed covers the whole of the physical world and the whole of human life that is lived in it, we packed Mrs Olive off barefoot and complaining to the kitchen, while we pored and planned the next three crowded weeks.

Macbeth has a very simple story line, lots of duologues for Him and Her, and no sub-plot, so it was easy to adapt. A short introduction, and only one linking narration were all that was needed by way of exposition. *The Merchant* was more difficult. It has sub-plots, changes of location, disguise, besides the tricky problem for me of switching from Bassanio to Shylock without the help of make-up.

I had just played the psychiatrist in Peter Shaeffer's astounding play *Equus*. In John Dexter's inspired production, unashamedly influenced by the Japanese Noh Theatre, an empty space with four benches was used to represent an office, a stable, a cinema, a street – anywhere at all, in fact, that the actors made of it. It was 'Theatre' at its most exciting. If an actor believes for example that a man in a mask with cages on his feet is a horse, then the audience believes he is a horse. If he picks up a non-existent 'prop', opens a non-existent door, or even speaks to a non-existent person, provided the actor believes what he is doing and meticulously mimes these activities, the audience will see what he wants them to see. Furthermore, it adds to the excitement to have to use their imagination.

We made a virtue of necessity. Since we would be doing two performances a day, sometimes at schools a hundred miles apart, with no stage-management or assistance of any kind, we decided to mime all props and stage furniture except for three chairs, which we estimated would not be impossible to find, even in the jungle. Only Marcel Marceau can look comfortable sitting on fresh air. (Which reminds me of a true story of the great mime artist. He was playing in Wolverhampton, dressed as Harlequin, his lithe body unhampered by the baggy androgynous costume, his face painted a classic chalk white. He had been caught in an imaginary tempest. He had climbed and fallen down imaginary stairs. He had taken a large imaginary dog for a walk. He had donned and doffed imaginary masks. Now Marcel Marceau could be a pretty funny name to some people, particularly in the less cosmopolitan and francophone parts of the world like Wolverhampton. A lady in the stalls had been watching Monsieur Marceau for quite half an hour in a stunned silence. Unable to keep her amazement to herself for a moment longer, she turned to her friend, who was equally boggled, and was heard, I'm told, even in the upper circle, to say, 'Doosn't she speak?')

However. We placed two chairs together as 'thrones' in *Macbeth*. We disposed them around as 'pillars' in *The Merchant*, and we imagined everything else that was essential. Tables, goblets, daggers, letters, swords, blood (there would be nowhere to wash it off), caskets, rings, bonds, and we took great delight in miming them all as well as we possibly could.

When Mrs Olive was 'doing', we got out from under her unforgettable feet and rehearsed in my place. When Katie was 'doing' for me, we rehearsed at Sue's. We directed each other most amicably, and felt wonderfully free from restraint.

There was still the problem of what to wear. As we were aiming at a performance and not simply an illustrated lecture, we wanted to suggest 'period', without holding the show up with changes of costume. The budget was tight and the clothes would have to be as light as possible, preferably in duplicate, and easily washed. Sue paraded in a few night-garments and kaftans and Laura

Ashley dresses, largely borrowed from friends, as her own wardrobe was as short on summerweight items as England has – until recently – been short on summer.

'That's fine for the sleep-walking scene, Sue, but it looks a bit comfortable for the banquet. And what about the trial scene?

You're *supposed* to fool everyone that you're a fella, and that neckline truly does wonders for your tits.'

'And what are *you* going to go as?' she asked, I thought, a little tartly.

'I don't know, but we don't want to look as if we've been rummaging about in a jumble sale, and are hoping for a prize.'

'This is a very expensive nightie!' she said. 'But I know what you mean.'

In the end, a girl-friend ran up a couple of identical black cotton dresses with elegant sleeves and a little train, both weighted with washers to make the flimsy material hang nicely. The washers went rusty and clanked a bit, but nobody minded.

For Lady Macbeth she wore a heavy black and gold belt, which she changed for Portia to a girdle with a lilac rose at her waist. She wore another rose on a band at her throat, and she looked all right. In the court scene, as Doctor Balthazar, she removed all the trimmings, and wore a simple black cloak (fixed with Velcro) and a pill-box on her head.

'Well, that's you fixed up. I can't get away with black jeans and an embroidered shirt now, can I?'

'Why not, darling?' She changed the rose at her throat to the other side and smiled at herself in the mirror. 'If we're both in black we'll look of a piece, and not just as if we're in fancy dress.'

'Yes, but you look so Elizabethan. I think it'll have to be tights, boots, and a cloak to give a bit of dash and cover the privates. My bum and my bulge would stop the show.'

'They're used to much worse than that over there, surely?'

'Not from people operating under the auspices of the British Council. What do you think of this for Shylock?'

I had been foraging in the Wig Department at Selfridge's, and had bought the cheapest black ladies' wig I could find. I pulled it over my ears and adjusted the angle in the mirror. It was not really long enough, but I reckoned that if I could steam out the huge bubble-curls, I could achieve the lank effect and the instant transformation I was seeking.

Sue was unconstructive. When she quietened down some ten minutes later, I thought she might need oxygen. She was gasping like a landed bloater, and the bosom of her nice new frock was soggy.

'You don't like it.'

'I *love* it! But if you wear it for Shylock, the tour's off.'

'Once the curls are straightened out...' But with awesome respect for Selfridge's and the Lithuanian Nuns or I.C.I. or whoever provides the hair, I found those curls to be indestructible. Steam them or stamp on them or put them through a mangle, they come out as pert and bubbly as the day they were first crimped.

'What shall I do? How can I be Bassanio one minute and Shylock the next without *any* change in appearance?' I was aware of sounding plaintive, but I could see no light at the end of the tunnel.

'Just act it, dear,' she said sincerely, without a trace of acid, and then went on to spoil it all by adding, 'Your Shylock would look overdone at The Palladium, but I love it just the same.'

I didn't take her advice. I bought a Jewish skull-cap and had a black silk square sewn onto it so that it covered my hair. The effect was more Muslem than Judaic, but at any rate it looked Middle-Eastern, and to my eyes at least quite definitely Semitic, and it gave me my instant transformation. By re-arranging my cloak (which was a Lebanese Abaya bought while I was playing in the Temple of Bacchus at the Baalbeck Festival and which I use as a dressing-gown) from a flamboyant, over-the-shoulder flourish for Bassanio, to a wrapped-up old-man's style for Shylock, I was well pleased with the result.

*

'You are, of course, going to the area in the world where there is the very highest health-risk,' the charming lady-doctor explained to us at the Air Terminal Inoculation Clinic, and as we saw the words forming on her lips we all three chorused in unison, 'The White Man's Grave.' We nodded with a wan smile. 'Yes, we know.'

'So you'd better have the lot, hadn't you?'

'How do you mean, "The Lot"?' Sue's knuckles gleamed livid against her Gucci bag.

'Well, you *have* to have cholera, yellow fever and typhoid, and smallpox of course, that goes without saying. You'll take your anti-malaria pills naturally, starting two weeks before you go, every day without fail, it's most important, and carry on taking them for at least a month after you get back – some doctors say two. Then I suggest you also have anti-tetanus, polio, and blogularwogularglobbywoggle' (at least, that's what it sounded like), which is for hepatitis. She sounded as if she was dispensing treats at a Sunday-school party. 'You ought to have that at the very last moment possible, as it's only effective for the first six weeks, and after that it's no good at all. How long are you going for?'

'About ten weeks.'

'Well, you ought to be half all right.'

'Hepatitis is the one where the syringe is a sort of petrol-pump and they just keep right on till they fill you up, isn't it?' Sue asked with a faint laugh.

'It is rather bigger than the others, but our nurses are very experienced and you'll hardly feel a thing. There might be a little discomfort for a few days afterwards, but – ' Her resigned shrug failed to put our minds at rest. 'I'll just write the list down for you. You pay first, and you'll have to come back in two weeks or so for boosters.'

'You mean we have to have them all *twice*?'

'I'm afraid so.' But she was listing away and didn't bother to look sympathetic.

'Now. We've got yellow fever, typhoid, cholera, polio, anti-tetanus and gammaglobbin. There we are!'

'Where do we buy them?'

'Just across the passage.'

*

We took a suitcase to Boots in Regent Street, and filled it with Paludrin (anti-malaria pills), salt-tablets (for heat-exhaustion), shampoo, wat r-purifying-tablets, toothpaste, Milton (for sterilising things), throat lozenges (we'd heard the dust could cause irritation), Sylvasun (we're both fair), Aspirin, Ambre Solaire, T.C.P., Elastoplast, Lomotol (liquid concrete for binding loose bowels), anti-histamine (bites), Kaolin, talcum, and about ten cannisters of insecticide and mosquito-repellant, and we began to feel there was no turning back.

*

An independent film producer got wind of our venture and was convinced it would make a documentary film. Sue and I were apprehensive about adding to our problems on the gruelling trip by having to film at the same time, but we were also sceptical about the project getting off the ground, as the insurmountable obstacle in the way of films being made is always money. Our producer, however, had assembled a formidable crew. The director was to be Peter Hall's assistant on the prize-winning

Akenfield. The camera-man and the sound-team had not only won awards for their work, they also spoke fluent French (which is the lingua franca in half of Cameroon), and had experience of filming on the Ivory Coast, which is, after all, roughly in the same climatic neck of the woods. As a result of this line-up, plus Sue and myself of course, and some reasonable dialogue contributed without charge by Shakespeare, the Cameroon cultural attaché got excited, and we were all invited to the Embassy in Holland Park to meet the ambassador for the express purpose of persuading him to put His Excellent hand deep into his big black Cameroonian pocket.

Socially the evening was a huge success. We had a foretaste of the charm and hospitality we were to meet later throughout West and Equatorial Africa, but the wheels of bureaucracy turn slowly, and though they were undoubtedly genuinely keen on the idea, there was simply not enough time, and 'Shakespeare Safari' was never made.

*

Three days to go. Though not exactly in a panic, I became erratic in my behaviour. Unsure of my priorities, I didn't know whether first to get the Trial Scene right, buy new underpants or make my will.

'We'll have to have a Final Dress,' Sue wheedled. She had been all packed and ready for a week, bills paid, and all sensible arrangements completed with cool efficiency. 'We've never done the whole programme full out. I have to time changing into my Portia bits without a mirror, and get used to these washers. If I flap my arms I could knock you out.'

'Then don't flap your arms,' I suggested. 'And if you can see a way of avoiding standing on my cloak when I let it down for Shylock, I'd be obliged.' I'd worn my Abaya a couple of times to get the feel of it and it had caused hitches. 'I've been positively dextrous in dodging your train.'

'There's more space at your place,' she said. So we cleared my sitting-room of all but three chairs, slipped into our costumes and took the 'phone off the hook.

'I think we look all right, don't you?'

'And your tights don't look a *bit* rude. Maybe your beard could do with a trim...but at least we look of a piece, don't you agree?'

'No one would guess it was all done for sixpence.'

Praise is essential in our business to instil confidence and to bring out the best; since we had only each other, a little self-congratulation must be excused.

'O.K., then check the clock.'

'All the stops out?'

'No holds barred!'

'Good luck.'

'Ladies and Gentlemen, Boys and Girls...' We launched into our preamble with gusto. The disadvantage of rehearsing in a moderate-sized room is that, although the floor-space may be adequate, when you are facing the imagined auditorium you find that your nose is one inch from the wall, and its hard to keep your mind on the play and not start worrying about the paintwork. We swept *Macbeth* along at a spanking pace however, though we were ultra-careful to enunciate clearly for our young African audiences.

The part of Macbeth requires huge energy and vocal attack, culminating in the great cry to battle when he hears that 'Birnam Wood is come to Dunsinane...'

ARM! ARM AND OUT! If this which he avouches does appear,
There is no flying hence – nor tarrying here.
I 'gin to be aweary of the sun
And wish th' estate of the world were now undone.
RING THE ALARUM BELL! Blow wind, come wrack,
At least we'll die with harness on our back.

I put my whole heart into it, all the rage and the crazed desolation of the warrior-king as he found himself trapped and cheated by the witches' devious prophecies.

At the end I was sweating (and this was a winter's day in England!), Sue was doggedly breathing through her nose, and dabbing at her brow with Kleenex. And we still had to do *The Merchant*. But the clock ticked on. We had no time for a rest, or coffee, or artificial respiration. With a damp squeeze of the hands we continued.

'And now, we're going to do *The Merchant of Venice*.'

There was a ring at the doorbell. I muttered to Sue, 'Keep going! I'm not expecting anyone.'

'Part Fairy-Tale, yet dealing with the harsh realities of money, and racial prejudice.'

There was another more insistent ring followed by loud knocking, which could not be ignored if the door was to remain on its hinges.

'Fuck!' I said. 'Check the clock,' and I strode furiously to the door in my borrowed boots, my Lebanese Abaya flying.

On the doorstep stood two uniformed policemen. One started to accost me, but his voice trailed away almost immediately, and they both stood silent as book-ends painfully taking in my unexpected garb.

'Yes?' I asked eventually, my anger instantly subsiding with the threat of apprehension. Could my tights conceivably be an infringement of the law? In my own home? They do it all the time at Covent Garden.

'We're investigating a complaint, sir,' the constable said, clearing his throat and failing to conceal his disdain. 'Your next-door neighbour says someone's being murdered.'

'Oh, for God's sake!' I calculated that the sight of Sue alive and well and equally extravagantly clad might convince them more than any protestations of mine that they had interrupted a highly respectable, creative dramatic work-out, and not some sordid case of wife-beating.

'Come in.'

After the introductions, I said, 'It's that "Call to arms" that did it', which made their blank looks even blanker. I realised it would be uphill work, but I explained as best I could. Sue made some coffee, and they seemed mollified though far from affable.

With further muttering about 'disturbing the peace' and some grovelling apologies from Sue and myself (we were all but on the eve of departure, and we were damned if we were going to be baulked at the last minute by a hysterical neighbour and two thick coppers) they finally left, casting a backward sneering glance at my flimsy nether garment.

✴

'May I have your attention please. The British Caledonian Flight Number 217 to Dakar, Freetown, and Accra has been delayed. The estimated time of departure is now 2200 hours. Will passengers booked on this flight please wait in the departure lounge for a further announcement.'

'WHAT?!'

'Twenty-two *hundred*?!'

'That's ten o'clock at night!'

Since we had risen at six to get to Gatwick by eight-thirty, as the flight had been scheduled to leave at 10 a.m., we were, to put it mildly, miffed. Having said our goodbyes, we felt no inclination to take the train back to Victoria and spend the day at home, neither coming nor going, in a lingering limbo.

'What do they expect us to *do* for twelve hours!' Sue was beginning to look tight-lipped. 'Wait in the departure lounge? Lounge! There isn't even a solitary hard-backed chair!'

At Gatwick there is nothing, but *nothing* to park one's butt on, and there is nothing like the prospect of a twelve-hour wait for draining the strength from the knees.

'We should have brought our shooting-sticks. The Safari's started sooner than I expected.'

'Oh well,' Sue said with resignation, and sank to a squatting position on the polished floor among the passing footwear, clutching her Marks and Spencer's plastic bag full of mosquito repellent and assorted rubbish. 'OooH!' She squirmed and started to laugh. 'It's warm!' So I kicked a couple of fag-ends out of the the way and joined her, though the under-floor heating was small comfort for our plight.

But British Caledonian came up trumps. They bussed us to The Last Post Hotel where we spent a pleasant day reading the papers, watching 'Jackanory', lingering over two edible meals, making the acquaintance of a civilised Swiss geologist, who was also bound for Freetown, all at the airline's expense, and getting mildly pissed at our own. We finally took off at 11 p.m. in a DC10 that had seen better days, but it *worked*. We were airborne and off at last.

'They say you can tell how long a man's been in Africa by what he does when a fly lands in his beer.'

23

THE BARD IN THE BUSH

Since we were by now, after all, a double-act, Sue fed me the cue conscientiously.

'How can you tell how long a man's been in Africa by what he does when there's a fly in his beer?'

'When he first arrives, he says, "Waiter! There's a fly in my beer." When he's been there a month, he picks it out himself. After that he drinks it fly and all.'

'I'll stick to champagne.'

'Champagne?' said a voice from above. We were still strapped in and dutifully sucking on our barley-sugar. On her way down the aisle snatching hand-luggage from the rack and pitching it onto the laps of protesting passengers, the stewardess had overheard us. 'Would you like some champagne? Oh, I've seen you on television, haven't I? "The Nearly Man"!' she said, grasping my shoulder fervently. 'Oh, you were wonderful!'

'No.' I think I looked wistful. 'I never did any of those, I'm afraid.'

'You *are* John Stride or something, aren't you?'

'Well, I'm something, but I'm not John Stride.' My laugh sounded shamelessly hollow.

'Oh, well, it can't be helped. What *is* your name?'

'John Fraser.'

She looked baffled. 'Oh. That can't be right.'

'I'm sorry.'

'Never mind. Hang on.'

We had no plans for doing anything else, so we waited while she went towards the nose, or mysterious part of the 'plane. She returned with the navigator who went wet round the mouth at the sight of Sue. We were whisked off to the crew's cramped quarters, plied with Dom Perignon and entertained like royalty for the rest of the sleepless night. Sue was cordially, though illicitly, invited to sit in the flight-deck for the touch-down and take-off at Dakar, and I was reluctantly allowed to take her place for the landing in Freetown. We soared down out of the night sky, sliding miraculously into the sparkling slot of the runway, just as the pale ghost of our first African dawn seeped stealthily through the banks of inky-black cloud.

Chapter One

Opening Night

Travelling to exotic countries by 'plane is a shock to the imagination if not to the system. If one could meander slowly through France, cross the Pyrenees into Spain, take a boat to Morocco, then brave the Sahara, one might be mentally prepared for the life and images of Africa that assault one's senses only six hours by air from one's own fireside.

Our stalwart geologist, with a car to meet him, had rescued us from the clutches of over-eager taxi-drivers, since, landing as we did over thirteen hours behind schedule, there was no one to meet us. We crossed a wide estuary on the car-ferry, the silhouette of gentle hills gradually brightening against the overcast sky, the chug of the engine the only sound to reach us across the still grey water. It was not as hot as we had expected, though we knew that once the sun was up no doubt we'd sizzle.

Freetown was in full swing in the cool of the morning. Tin-shack markets and little stalls set up along the roadside selling beer and Fanta and cheap cigarettes. Mounds of scraped oranges for sucking. Cooked meat on skewers and trays of unappetising morsels. Mangy dogs and wrecks of cars and unfamiliar smells. Poverty and squalor, but some beautiful faces and bodies, some clothed in rags torn across one shoulder, which in Europe would be seductive. Ebony cherubs wrapped astride their mothers' backs, heads lolling, tiny toes pointing to the sky. The brilliant colours of gowns and bandannas glowing against the dark skin. The sparkling teeth. And everywhere, men, women and children carrying

pots and basins and firewood and sideboards and sewing mach-
ines and everything portable under the Equatorial sun on their
heads. Scrawny vultures wheeling over the meat-market. Croco-
diles of children in immaculate uniforms trooping off to school,
their books, of course, in boxes borne aloft. A lady having her
hair styled like the Bride of Frankenstein, while a ferocious baby
snapped at her purple rubbery dug. Muslems pouring out of the
mosque in flowing white gowns and embroidered caps. Ample
bosoms and rippling torsos and epic bums rolling under lurid
cotton wrappers. Naked children tumbling in the dust. Pools of
deepest shadow lit by disembodied eyes gazing languorously out
at the teeming street. An old hag with flat triangular breasts flapping like bunting. Stalls with sandals and banks of shoes and boots
-- status symbols now, where all used to go barefoot. Everywhere
the erect, strong bodies seemed to proclaim their 'returned-slave'
ancestry. First, selection of the fittest, then survival in the slave
ships, there *and* back. The emphasis on physical strength is reflected in their language, which is evolved from pidgin English.
In Krio, the traditional greeting is 'How de body?', and the hoped-
for reply is 'De body fine!'

'That's the City Hotel where Graham Greene wrote *The Heart
of the Matter*.' (Sue had the book in her suitcase to re-read on the
spot.) It is a marvellously sleazy, once dignified building, where
expatriots still congregate for lunch-time refreshments before driving off to eat in the newer air-conditioned establishments. 'They
did up the bar a few years ago, and everyone was so upset they
had to do it down again.'

For the first week we were staying just outside the city at the
Cape Sierra, a holiday hotel at the tip of a long peninsula jutting
out into the bay. The rooms were air-conditioned and the staff
was smiling and our first performance wasn't till the next day.
There was a five-mile sweep of dazzling white beach, empty save
for two lines of fishermen hauling in their nets beside a sickle-
shaped coracle.

'Oh darling...' is what Sue says when she is lost for words, and
she said it.

The slightly murky pool was surrounded by date-palms and a
motley selection of caricature colonials and youngsters on pack-

age tours playing ping-pong and turning various shades of puce.

'This isn't too hard to bear, is it? Mind you, it's the only period of luxury we'll have, so let's enjoy it while we can', which may have been niggardly of me but forewarned is forearmed.

We were taken to our first 'venue' at the top of a pine-clad hill overlooking the whole of Freetown. Vultures floated lazily through the shifting blue haze from the cooking-fires, and the reggae music blaring from a loudspeaker far below was muted.

The British Council Hall was quite beyond our expectations, in an elegant, recently completed building, cool and well appointed, with seating for four hundred, dressing-rooms with all mod. cons, a stage equipped with curtains and lights, and two smiling helpers to operate them, Gabriel and Big Ba.

'You'll be playing here all this week – just one performance every day at six,' Alan, Our Scotsman from the British Council informed us. 'I hope it's all right.'

'It's wonderful!' Sue beamed. She clambered up onto the stage and bellowed at the top of her voice, 'They met me in the day of success and I have learned by the perfectest report they have more in them than mortal knowledge!' which gave Alan a nasty turn.

'Trying out the acoustics,' I explained with a smile, then I asked Sue, 'Is it all right?'

'Feels fine. How does it sound?'

'Hang on – I'll go to the back.'

'WHEN I BURNED IN DESIRE TO QUESTION THEM FURTHER THEY MADE THEMSELVES AIR INTO WHICH THEY VANISHED...'

'Hold it!' I yelled. 'You can take it down to half, dear. Can't you see the windows rattle? There won't be so much echo when the hall's full.' I suddenly had a worrying thought. 'Will it be full, Alan?'

'Oh, God yes! Oh, def'nately,' Alan assured me in the comforting accent of our home town. 'Shakespeare's part of their curriculum, John. Here's a list of the schools...Oh, it'll be full all right. They're all dead keen to pass their exams. Often a whole family scrimps and saves just to put one kid through school, you see, so they're all dead keen. Dead keen. You wait!'

'That explains why they're so proud of their uniforms – and so immaculate!'

'Oh, they're neatly turned out, all right. Sometimes jist the one pair o' breeks, mind, but they're whipped off and washed the minute they get in the door. And that's without plumbing, often as not, with their Mammies humphin' the water all the way from the well.' He stubbed out his fourth half-smoked cigarette, and placed it in the ashtray beside the others in a neat little row, a curious habit of this meticulous man.

Sue was arranging the curtains at the back with the help of Big Ba, to make us an imposing entrance.

'Will they understand the plays? I mean, English is difficult enough, but Elizabethan English...'

'Oh, don't worry. They'll have studied at least one of the plays. English is often their third language, mind you.'

'Their third?'

'Oh aye. They speak their tribal one first – Limba, Temne or whatever, but they all learn Krio. That's the lingua franca here, you understand. The folk are called Creole, but the language is called Krio.'

'It's sort of pidgin, isn't it?'

'Not a bit of it! No, no. Not any more. It started off on the plantations, of course, but now it's a language on its own. A few recognisable words here and there mebbe, but that's all. Most urban Sierra Leonians at any rate speak a bit of English.'

'But Shakespeare...'

'Oh listen. Jist wait and see. They like to enjoy themselves.'

Which sounded ominous.

*

'Merde!' I gave Sue a friendly kick and a fairly dry spit on the shoulder. These unsavoury practices had been picked up through years of working in the theatre, where 'Good Luck!' seems inadequate either to calm first-night nerves or to convey heartfelt sympathy. 'I've put the champagne in the cistern, as there's only "hot" and "hotter" in the sink.'

When she hugged me I could feel her trembling.

'Just enjoy it!'

'If we could only start!'

It was nearly half-past six. Alan had warned us that punctuality was not high on their list of priorities, and the Minister of Culture and one school had yet to arrive. Sue started to pace the floor, quietly clanking and wringing her hands. She muttered, 'Was the hope drunk wherein you dressed yourself? And has it slept since?' 'AERH!!' I yelled. 'Out! Out you go!'

In a superstitious profession, the one abiding, never-flouted custom, observed universally by the sceptical and the superstitious alike, is to refrain from quoting *Macbeth* in the dressing-room. This curious state of affairs springs no doubt from the long, bloodstained history of productions of this play.

Shakespeare dwells on darkness in *Macbeth* more than in any of his other works, not simply as a symbol – the 'forces of darkness', the 'evil influences' and the supernatural are of course of paramount importance to the plot – but also because the play was the first one that he wrote to be *played* in the dark, by candlelight. His previous plays were written for the Globe, where the actors performed in daylight in the open air. For the first time in England, a Scottish king sat on the throne, James the First, and Sixth of Scotland. The play was written for him, hence the Scottish setting, and the character of 'Banquo', who was to 'father a long line of kings' (the Stuarts), was James's supposed, though mythical, forebear. *Macbeth* was written specifically to be played first at the court, and later at Blackfriars, where Shakespeare, who had by this time assumed the mantle of impresario on top of that of actor and playwright, had recently acquired a new theatre. The witches, the apparitions, and all the magical effects, would clearly work better and be much more frightening by candlelight, as would the terrible murders of Duncan, Banquo and Lady Macduff – and the sleep-walking scene. To people used to watching plays presented in bright sunlight, in the irreverent day-time bustle of which a typical Elizabethan audience was composed – orange-girls and whores and young bloods greeting friends and drinking ale and sack – when *Macbeth* was first performed in the flickering half-gloom it must have been startling and chilling and utterly revolutionary.

It is a combination of the dark, the special effects, and the violence which has exposed performers in *Macbeth* throughout the years to accidents not associated with other plays. There are folklore tales of actual death by sword or retracting dagger which failed to retract. The period of the action being the eleventh century, the battle scenes are fought with mighty broadswords, not the light épée of the *Hamlet* period, so wounds and split heads are frequent. Witches are constantly scraping shins or even breaking bones as the 'air into which they vanish' is usually pitch-darkness, and perhaps through a trap or off a high rostrum. 'Apparitions' have been known to pile up most corporeally in the wings, spikey crowns endangering unseeing eyeballs and royal sceptres goosing Stuart monarchs feeling for an exit through the black tabs.

Among actors, the taboo surrounding the play is so strong that many refuse to quote from it anywhere. If you are rehearsing it or playing it, colleagues consider you are pretty well sunk anyway. It has even acquired a second title so that it can be referred to without fear of something unspeakable happening, which is 'The Scottish Play'. To quote it in the *dressing-room* is the most heinous crime it is possible to commit in the theatre.

'OUT!' I yelled again, and Sue visibly blanched.

'It was under my breath!' she protested.

'I *heard* you!'

She meekly left the room, turned round three times, and knocked to be re-admitted. I relented, and she came in abject with contrition, uttered a filthy four-letter word, and the nameless curse was counteracted by good magic. All this from two people who heedlessly walk under ladders, who spill salt and break mirrors without a morbid thought, who are both agnostic, and I believe rational human beings. How could we scoff at the amazing beliefs we were to hear of later, of Secret Societies and their abominable rites...

'I wish we knew how they're going to react...'

'They can't be worse than English kids.'

'Can't they?'

'Those school matinees at the Vic...snotty-nosed little monsters. They were great fun, just the same.'

'It's all raving madness.'

'Yep.'

'I don't mean getting nervous for a bunch of school-kids. I

mean doing it at all. What are we doing all dressed up pretending to be the King and Queen of bloody Scotland in the middle of Africa! Why should they care?'

'Look. Shakespeare's performed in translation all over the world. That proves he's universal. I've seen two black *Macbeths* to date. The Zulu *Umabata* on the stage, and the Xhosa film, *Mxhosa*. Nobody *told* them to do those versions, they just see the parallels with their own history of tribal wars, ruthless ambition and witchcraft...There's the Japanese *Throne of Blood* too. I think *Macbeth* is perhaps the most universal of all the plays. There are musicals galore of *Romeo and Juliet* and *The Taming of the Shrew* and *The Comedy of Errors* and *The Merchant* – the list is endless – and operas in every language. His impartial understanding of the entire range of human nature, from paupers to princes, his wisdom, his humanity, his wit, and his dazzling use of language – it applies to the whole human race. I think, as a child, Shakespeare almost – no, I think he did. He really did.'

'Did what?'

'Changed my life.'

'How?'

'Well, we had a great teacher, certainly. And you'll never guess the plays we studied.'

'*Macbeth* and *The Merchant of Venice*.'

'Right.'

'So did we.'

'Plus ça change, plus c'est la même chose.'

'Don't you get Froggy with me.'

'Anyway – it didn't make me want to be an actor, or anything, but he was the first writer I had ever read that I was aware was monumental. He's awe-inspiring – as if the Bible had been written by one man, except that Shakespeare had no axe to grind.'

Alan pounded sweating up the stairs and said, 'O.K.? They're all here. We can start now. I've told Ba to stand by on the curtain. I'm looking forward to this, honest to God. Good luck!' And he had gone, and we were on and the hall was packed and they were as quiet as mice, and the mezzin calling the faithful to prayer in a distant mosque should have been incongruous and somehow wasn't.

When playing to school audiences in England, if you want a sure-fire laugh, mention sex or bodily functions. We were a little apprehensive about lines like, 'I have given suck, and know how tender 'tis to love the babe that milks me.' I watched in trepidation in the wings as Sue approached a danger zone...

In her first soliloquy, she was conjuring the spirits of evil to strengthen her resolve to murder Duncan, and clear the way for Macbeth to grab the Throne of Scotland.

> Come you spirits
> That tend on mortal thoughts, unsex me here;

Not a titter.

> And fill me from the crown to the toe top full
> Of direst cruelty. Make thick my blood,
> Stop up the access and passage to remorse
> That no compunctious visitings of nature
> Shake my fell purpose, nor keep peace between
> The effect and it!

'Here it comes,' I thought. 'They're going to whoop and jeer and start throwing the furniture...'

Sue plunged to her knees and kneaded her shapely bosom, just as we had rehearsed it.

'Come to my woman's breasts and take my milk for gall...'

What had happened? You could hear a pin drop! Peeping through the curtains, I could see hundreds of bright eyes, which was all I *could* see in the darkened auditorium, and they were filled with rapt attention. Not a snigger or a knowing glance or a nudge to a neighbour. Nothing.

With hindsight, we realised that there is nothing remotely prurient about mammary glands in a country where one is metaphorically slapped in the teeth by monumental boobies round every corner.

'We're home and dry!' I thought, as I made my entrance amid a hushed expectancy.

'My dearest love!'

Sue ran to welcome me, and I embraced her passionately. We played the ensuing dialogue in each other's arms, but not a word was heard. The shrieks of laughter scared the vultures off the roof.

We disentangled ourselves, but only when we had finally retreated to arms length did the commotion subside. It could hardly fail to penetrate that tits and all were fine, but kissing and cuddling were definitely out.

'Oh, God. Now it's our turn.' Sue's shoulders were shaking. I opened my mouth to speak, and though I managed to control my facial muscles, what emerged was a strangled but quite audible guffaw.

We were in the throes of an affliction peculiar to our profession called 'corpsing'. Anyone who remembers schooldays – a humourless teacher, perhaps, with his shirt-tail peeping through his flies, or a funeral service, when weeping heads are lowered in prayer and one's deaf aunt noisily passes wind – will understand our predicament. It can be set off by something which in normal circumstances would scarcely raise a tired smile. It only happens in the theatre when one is expected to be serious or sad or sinister or profound. You never want to laugh if it is permissible to do so, but when you *daren't* the impulse is irresistible.

(One of the most distinguished young actresses in England suffers so acutely from this disease that she was approached by her director's wife – also an actress, with a well-earned reputation for concealing her malice behind a gracious smile. 'Darling!' said the director's wife, 'there is a very good cure for "corpsing", don't you know it?' 'I wish I did,' said the actress, shame-faced. 'Just think,' said the director's wife, 'just think of getting the sack!')

I made a detour round the stage taking deep breaths and surreptitiously wiping the tears from my face. I could just about go on if I avoided looking into her eyes.

'But what about Bassanio?' I was thinking wildly. 'Turn you where your lady is and claim her with a loving kiss...' 'How do I get round *that*?'

When we came to it later in the evening one could feel their gleeful anticipation mounting. It was almost unfair to cheat them, but it would have stopped the show. I stood where I could just about reach Sue if I leant a little, and 'the kiss' I claimed Portia with was a very frightened peck on the top of her outstretched middle finger. Bedlam was avoided.

Lesson One. A public display of affection between the sexes is considered both weak and highly indecorous.

✳

We were lying by the pool feeling well content. Our opening night, Alan had assured us, had been a triumph, in spite of the ribald response to our first and only embrace, and the Minister of Culture and other Distinguished Adults who had been present at the reception after the performance had all made convincing noises of appreciation. There was no doubt in our own minds that the children had understood us and enjoyed the plays, which was a considerable relief. They had stayed at the end to ask intelligent and searching questions.

'What is the significance of the supernatural in *Macbeth*?'

'Bassanio is unworthy of Antonio's love. Discuss.'

'Are you lovers?'

'If you're not, how can you kiss?'

Apart from a radio-interview we had the whole day free. I was already as brown as a lobster, so I was lurking beneath a big blue brolly sucking coca-cola through a straw, thoroughly at peace with this strange hot, sticky corner of the world.

'What do you make of "the Illustrated Man" and "the Second-Last Tango"?' I was referring to some fellow guests who, like us, were availing themselves of the poolside amenities.

'The Illustrated Man' lolled on a chair-bed, his bloated belly bulging over his baggy trunks. There was not a visible part of the rolling acres of his flesh which was not covered in tattoos and writing. Hearts and dragons and naked damsels adorned his pendulous chest; snakes writhed up through the jungle of black hairs on his massive arms; the illegible mottoes and slogans in purple and red and black pricked into the skin of his mottled thighs would have been reading-matter for a week, if one could have deciphered them.

'The Second-Last Tango' was dressed, if you can call it that, in a zebra-striped and glittering-gold confection, which seemed to my unprudish view to be not only immodest but padded, and was alternately flexing his pectorals by dynamic tension, then pummelling his flaccid calves with the edge of his heavily-ringed hand.

He was well over forty, with crudely dyed black curls clustering round his shoulders, and he sported a rich tan and a ring in one ear.

'They must be the Lebanese Alan was talking about.' 'Syrians', Graham Greene calls them in *The Heart of the Matter*. Whatever their origin, these pale-skinned Arabs have business tied up in Freetown, and are consequently unpopular.

'Do you fancy an exhausted totter down to the beach?' I suggested. Lying prone in the sun is fine if you're convalescing, but I find it short on stimulation and I get burnt. Sue on the other hand

is content to toast, particularly as we had made discreet inquiries by this time, so that we knew that our first week at the Cape Sierra would be the only part of our trip which would approximate to a holiday.

'We can have a swim before lunch.'

We picked our way through a grove of palms, past importunate traders eager to foist on us leather goods and ivory necklaces and wicked-looking spears. Two solitary women ambled along the empty beach balancing trays of fruit atop their bandannaed heads. Labourers building an extension onto the Beach Casino worked, as they do everything, at a dignified tropical pace, and the sweat gave their skins the gleam of patent leather.

'They can have Acapulco. This'll do me,' Sue spluttered, coming up for air after a most accomplished demonstration of the dog-paddle.

'I thought you could swim like an Olympic athlete! What about that film you did in Tobago?'

'That was a double, silly. But I can do an elegant side stroke,' and she did.

'I think you've won some admirers.'

Drawn, perhaps, by the prospect of watching Sue emerge from the waves like Aphrodite in a wet bikini, 'the Syrians' had followed us onto the beach.

'They don't half look sinister.' Sue was genuinely alarmed. 'We're out of earshot of everybody if they try anything funny.'

'Don't worry. They wouldn't dare do anything with me here.'

'Darling, either one of them could eat you for breakfast.'

'Thanks. It's nice to know you have such confidence in me.'

'My God! They're coming in!'

'Why not, for Heaven's sake! They're entitled to have a swim!' But something about their purposeful single-mindedness made me nervous.

'They're coming straight for us!'

Leaving a wake like a speedboat, the two men bore down on us in a churning flurry of tattooed arms and ringed fingers.

'Dog-paddle for your life!' I hissed at Sue, but our aquatic prowess was no match for that of our pursuers.

'CHOOOOOM!' 'the Illustrated Man' boomed at us.

'Choom! Can't you speak Arabic?' I asked Sue irascibly, but they were upon us and we were trapped.

'Ey, choom!' A thick fist grabbed at me, and I found my nose flattened against a hairy nipple surrounded by a scene from Hieronymus Bosch in scarlet and bruise-blue. 'Would you laik to coom to a party?' he asked in the thickest Lancashire accent I have heard outside Blackpool, which is where, it transpired, he came from.

'You're English!' My laugh sounded distinctly high-pitched. Sue swallowed a mouthful, and started to cough terminally and turn blue.

'Yeah! I'm Jack, and this is Bernie,' he said, introducing his Dago companion who now looked like a water spaniel, as his perm had gone frizzy from the swim.

Over a beer by the pool they explained ruefully that they were all that remained of a team of six professional wrestlers who had come out from England to entertain the Sierra Leonians. They had been a qualified disaster. It was hard to look surprised.

'Bluidy Joongle-Boonies!' Jack spat with disgust. 'They joost doan't knoa aout abaout the noable art of oonarmed cambaht! Bluidy ignerant, thaht's wot they are. Joost doan't want to knoa, they doan't. We're goan bahck oahm Fraiday, boot we thought we'd 'ave a party first. Thursday naight. At t'laighthouse. Are you coomin'?'

'Thank you, Jack,' which seemed a modest enough name for some of his flamboyant profession, and a man of such amazing proportions and patina, 'we'd love to.' But Sue didn't look so sure.

*

Our radio-interview took place in what looked like a disused railway station about to be demolished, alive with vendors selling oranges and fags and nuts from wicker trays. On 'the platform' there were lines of patient, strong-smelling youths lounging like a dole queue against the peeling walls, waiting for God knows what. In 'the waiting-room' we were introduced to the entire staff, announcers, disc-jockeys, secretaries and technicians. They were oblivious of their unsalubrious surroundings, and they appeared to be having a riotous party. They were all crisp and clean and affable to a quite euphoric degree.

Our interviewer was dressed like a fashion-plate, with a Dynatron Digital strapped to his elegant wrist the size of my portable telly. Just as he was about to start, a fuse blew. In the radio-station, not his watch. As it took two hours to mend, we had time to get acquainted.

'I would not presume to ask you this, John, if we were broadcasting to the nation, you know, man? But seeing as we have the time at our disposal due to this unfortunate little set-back, to have a chin-wag and to put the record straight, I would like to put to you a very serious question. You are under no obligation to come clean with me if you do not have the urge.'

'Sure, go ahead.'

'I have been reading your biographical details which your British Council sponsors have been kind enough to slip to me this morning, and I observe with interest from these details that you have written a play for the live theatre, and to this dramatic work you have given the title of *Cannibal Crackers*.'

I nodded modestly.

'Is this work that you have composed –' Though the wires were dead, in a conditioned reflex he put his hand over the microphone and lowered his voice to a conspiratorial whisper, 'Is it about cannibalism?'

'No, of course not. It's a metaphorical title, you know? Dog eat dog, that sort of thing.' I laughed, but he remained deadly serious.

'Ah, it's metaphorical. I see. I was perturbed to think that in England, you... It's a terrible thing, to be a cannibal. There is nothing worse anywhere in the whole world. I am happy to know that your play for the live theatre does not deal with such a subject. Those things are best to remain unmentionable... John! We'll say no more. I will come to London one day, and you will introduce me to Matt Monro.'

The fuse was fixed at last, for the air-conditioner rattled back into life. We were grateful because the room was stifling, though the atmosphere in the other sense had become puzzlingly chilly.

＊

'Second nights' are always an anti-climax. We were late starting, as the hall had been occupied until the last minute by a meeting of 'Women's Lib.', which is not as incongruous as it seems, for the movement in Sierra Leone owes nothing to the inspiration of Germaine Greer. Far from being down-trodden, the women are very powerful. In the markets, there is hardly a man to be seen, either buying, which is not surprising, or selling, which is. Meat, vegetables, fish, fruit, spices, hardware, clothes, crockery – all the tradespeople are women, young babies suckling or asleep on their mothers' backs, while the older children toddle among the maze of stalls unhampered either by clothes or parental restraint. In a country which abounds in secret societies, where almost every adult belongs to one or other of them (with names like 'The Leopard', 'Bundu', 'The Baboon'), the women's societies are the most feared and respected. Like a trade-union, the society gives them solidarity and bargaining power. Young initiates are frequently to be seen walking arrogantly along the road in twos and threes, their faces ghostly with white clay, which proclaims to all their recent graduation to the arcane mysteries exclusive to their group.

Our second show was over. One school had failed to turn up, as their teacher had died. ('Any excuse!' Sue said.) Since we had abandoned clinches our small audience was beautifully behaved. I was disappointed in one respect, however. They failed to find my 'Shylock' a character of tragic stature. I only had to don my headgear and assume my old-man's posture and gait for them all to split their sides and make the rafters merrily ring.

'I'm not *playing* for laughs. You do realise that, don't you?' I said to Sue as we removed our sodden costumes, while gulping greedily at a litre bottle of lukewarm 'Star', the local Lager which does *much* more than refresh the parts other beers cannot reach.

'I know you're not, love. They like acting being seen to be done, that's all.'

'You think I'm overdoing it?'

'Well, I wouldn't call it subtle, but – can I have the powder?'

She turned the talcum upside down above her head and disappeared in a white cloud, from which her voice emerged like God's to Moses from the Burning Bush. 'When you don't have make-up, you have to change yourself somehow, I quite see that. But do you have to make such faces?'

'Faces! I don't make faces! I've *never* made faces! It all comes from inside. If it *shows* on my face, that's fine. That's as it should be. But I don't start from my face and work in. I work from the inside out. You try. Go on then – *you* be Shylock. Just show me. You try being a bitter, twisted old man *without* making faces.'

'They love it, darling, you know they do. I shouldn't change a thing.'

'I don't make faces.'

Lesson two. It's probably self-defence, but Africans have no sympathy for the underdog. They also like acting 'being seen to be done', so I had to learn to live with the laughter.

*

How can I describe the Saturnalia that 'The Illustrated Man' had organised for his 'friends' at The Lighthouse? A spirited filly out of Creole Mammy by Lancashire Lad...Due to a perfectly understandable misunderstanding, we were unforgiveably late. Our Limba driver first drove us miles out to sea along a narrow causeway, his hooded eyes tactfully concealing his doubts about our sanity when we had gaily asked, 'Can you take us to The Lighthouse Arthur?' at eleven o'clock at night. It was not till we had arrived at a twenty-foot-high iron-mesh fence, which only just held in two Alsatians baring their dripping fangs and snarling hideously in the intermittent flash of the sweeping beam, that it occurred to us that our rendezvous with Jack had no connection except in name, nor indeed (with the mountainous breakers pounding about our axle in the emptiness of the open Atlantic) even any physical proximity to this solitary warning-system for passing sea-traffic.

The misunderstanding thus conclusively cleared up, once we had gained terra firma again we had been guided to the restaurant by a garrulous young buck of whom we had made inquiries on the road. Distrustful of our finding it on our own, he had jumped in and driven miles out of his way to deliver us safely, demanding the story of our lives as we went.

'Ey, man! You give me tickets – I come to see your show! I'm partial to de singin' and de dancin'.' He blithely accepted our offer of a drink for his kindness, so we had all four decanted ourselves into the foetid gloom of the night club.

We located our host, conveyed our apologies, and were led like a sacrifice to a terrace overlooking the sea. Jack had arranged four long tables in a square, where all his guests were seated and already showing signs of over-indulgence. Dancing on the table is all very fine, but when the plates have not been cleared, and some of the more dogged diners are still trying to unskewer their kebabs and toss the salad in an advanced stage of inebriation, it could be ill-advised, not to say dangerous. Though the dancer was formidably beautiful in the manner of a Russian weight-lifter, I have to admit that her grinds were more effective than her bumps.

'Joost introdyoose yourselves, woan't you?' Jack said, squeezing us in between a coolly elegant European lady and a lecherous Sierra Leonian who had eyes for nothing but the lady on the table, and whose beard was consequently quite saturated with saliva.

'Will you 'ave room?'

'Oh, we have plenty of room thank you, Jack.'

'Noa! Room! Would you laik soom room? *Jamayaca* Room!'

'Oh! Sue?'

'There's some wine here, Jack. That'll be lovely.'

'Hey DELAILAH!' Jack bellowed. 'GET YER BIG BLACK ARSE OFF T'BLUIDY TAYBLE, and let me mookers get their chompers raound soom nosh, for Chraist's sayke. We'll 'ave plenty taime for depravity layter. The naight's a poop!'

The night was an elderly dog when Jack stripped to his trunks in the square formed by the tables and beat his decorated chest like a gorilla. He was joined in a trice by Bernie, flinging his shirt and trousers over his shoulder as he jumped over the debris of Kus-Kus and Angel Delight, and before anyone at this befuddled hour had time to grasp what was happening the two wrestlers were entwined in a thumping, grunting, belligerent embrace.

Jack certainly gave the impression that this bizarre cabaret was impromptu. But could it be coincidence that the tables formed an adequate ring? And do they habitually wear their scanty finery as underwear? There was something almost noble about their child-like desire to exit with applause. Their professional engagements might have been disastrous, but alcohol in abundance was lubricating the slipway to give them a send-off to remember.

A little starveling of a man in grubby cotton trousers and a jockey's hat could not be restrained from undertaking to referee. His gaze was erratic. Whether it was due to 'room' or a congenital defect, one eye looked east while the other looked west. Whether he was familiar with the finer points of this most puzzling and histrionic of sports was questionable and unimportant, for he more than made up for any areas of ignorance with his enthusiasm. He cavorted amid the thrashing limbs like a monkey on a stick, counting fervently whenever there was a lull in the action, and screeching with laughter at the agonised expressions we assumed they were assuming, for as far as one could tell it was more of a choreographed acrobatic dance than a contest.

Bernie was 'the Hero' and Jack 'the Villain'. They knew how to manipulate their audience, shamelessly arousing its emotions. Jack turned on the crowd when it jeered at him as if he would smash every one of us to kingdom come, while we responded with an angry chorus of mock-hatred. Bernie appealed to us, as if he were a man grossly wronged. For men of their age and weight they managed a few surprising throws, some hilarious positions, and some truly inspired facial expressions.

'*That's* making faces!' I yelled at Sue above the din. 'P'raps I can pick up a few tips!'

The whole uproarious restaurant pressed around cheering and booing and banging the tables. When Bernie was declared the winner by universal demand, the bedlam knew no bounds. Jack acted huffy for five seconds flat, then with a tumultuous whoop he threw himself into the air in a final somersault, wobbling all over like a ludicrous painted baby. They were submerged in a black and white pyramid of hugging and back-slapping and kissing and cuddling.

They were redeemed.

*

It was almost morning, but we could not tear ourselves away from the enthralling woman sitting opposite us. We had sent Arthur home, and Alison had made a detour to her house in the mountains on our way back to the hotel. The night was cool, and being the dry season there were no mosquitoes to prevent us from having a cold drink on her terrace overlooking the estuary. The sky was black and starless, but the outline of the unkempt palms sweeping down to the sea was faintly etched against a paleness in the East. Only the wheezing of the old night-watchman punctuated the non-stop chirruping of the cicadas.

She must have been fifty, but she looked younger: handsome rather than beautiful, with chic and intellect and such an air of good breeding that even if we hadn't been told that she was the secretary to the president she would have commanded our attention. Placed next to her at dinner, we had all 'clicked'. The ambience at The Lighthouse being rather too exuberant for serious conversation, we had welcomed the chance to become acquainted.

'What on earth were you doing at Jack's party?' Sue asked, keeping a weather eye open for a moth the size of a fist which her X-ray vision had located feeding peacefully on the potted Pride of Barbados.

'I was asked.'

'Do you know him?'

'Never met him before in my life. I was buying some tanning-cream at the Cape Sierra – there isn't much demand for it in the town you understand – and he came straight up to me and said, "Would you laik to coom to my party?" and I said, "Yes, please." I like him. He has a heart the size of a Blackpool tram.'

'It's true. He just invited everybody he liked the look of.'

'Best way to have a party. Proper entertaining can be so dull. I haven't enjoyed myself so much in years.'

'He'll go home happy.'

'Do you mind being asked about your work?' I said.

'Not at all. Few people are interested.'

'I was told you saved the president's life.'

She smiled, then sighed.

'I did. Inadvertently. Before coming to Sierra Leone, I was secretary to President Nkrumah of Ghana. He is irreplaceable. I loved him very deeply. My heart broke when he died.'

She was nothing if not forthright. Why, one wondered, should African presidents employ a middle-aged English woman in such a position of confidence in preference to an African? Her story, perhaps, reveals one of the reasons...

'I call this little episode "How I carried the can".' She brought herself back to the more immediate past.

It was an ordinary day at Government House in Freetown. Siaka Stevens was not yet president but prime minister, and Alison was working as his secretary. During the course of the morning she felt the call of nature, and the architecture of the building is such that she had to go out onto the balcony and pass three offices before reaching the loo. On arriving, she found it occupied. She was dawdling and only just beginning to march on the spot when she thought she heard fireworks. Leaning over the balcony in the expectation of finding some celebration in progress, she was appalled to see in the distance troops advancing in armoured cars, blazing away with machine-guns at the very spot where she was standing. There had been no warning of an impending 'coup', but expected or un, it was happening. Running for her life along the whole length of the balcony amidst another burst of gunfire, she dived back into her office. Reckoning that the louvred-glass windows offered scant protection, she crouched on the floor behind a filing cabinet and pulled the 'phone down beside her. It was still working.

The troops surrounded the building, calling through loud-hailers for Siaka Stevens to give himself up. Alison dialled all the friends and colleagues whose numbers she could remember, giving them all the information she could, and begging them to do their utmost to save the prime minister and the dire situation in which they found themselves. Meanwhile the needs of her bladder, aggravated without doubt by the circumstances, became insistent. Scanning the office, she could find no receptacle remotely suitable for her purpose. Two slim pencil containers, several flat filing-trays, a measly couple of very small ashtrays, a wicker waste-paper basket, two cups and saucers, a jar of Nescafé, an electric kettle, a teaspoon, a sugar-bowl and a large tin of 'Needo' dried milk. 'Needo!' she exclaimed, in the manner of Archimedes in his bath, and immediately crawled to the table to retrieve the tin. Emptying the contents into the waste-paper basket, with a few contortions she at last succeeded in relieving herself. Her main preoccupation then became what to do with it. She would have liked to shout 'Gardey-loo!' and tip it over the heads of the men with the machine-guns below the balcony, but she suspected it would not douse their hostility. She settled for putting it outside the door in a passage, hoping that no one would mistake the contents for Fanta or palm-wine, and – thirst being what it is under siege – quaff it, without first testing.

But there was an eerie silence in the passage. All the Creole staff had disappeared. She later discovered that the soldiers had allowed them to leave the premises peaceably, for it was only Siaka

Stevens's blood they were after. She called his name as loudly as she dared, but there was no answer. Perhaps he was dead...She crawled along the passage avoiding the broken glass, though she was cut without feeling it. The door to Mr Stevens's office stood ajar. It was riddled with bullets, but it was empty and the only blood to be seen was her own. The strange silence was broken by the sound of her name blasting through the loud hailer. 'MISS ARMITAGE? MISS ARMITAGE! COME OUT OF THE BUILDING! COME OUT OF THE BUILDING NOW! YOU WILL BE QUITE SAFE. MISS ARMITAGE! MISS ARMITAGE...' Alison had no idea whether her employer was alive or dead, captured or free, but she was now convinced that she alone was left in the building.

Being a woman of great fastidiousness, she carefully put the lid back on the Needo tin. Screwing up her courage, she took her handbag in one hand, 'the can' in the other. She walked slowly because her knees were trembling so hard she had difficulty remaining upright. She descended the stairs and stepped out into the blinding sun where a dozen machine-guns were pointing at her. They kept the guns trained on her while she got into her car with her bag and the can and drove away.

The coup was abortive. Siaka Stevens had been smuggled out by a loyal bodyguard under the very noses of the rebels. When the revolt was squashed a few days later, he returned to power as President of the Republic.

' "I owe my life to you, Alison," he said to me. "If they had stormed the building, I would have been a dead man."

' "Why didn't they?" I asked him.

' "Because of you. If they had killed an English woman, there would have been an international incident." ' She laughed.

'But I'm quite a good secretary as well!'

As she drove us back through the waking town, she said, 'You have to meet Michael. I'm going there for lunch on Saturday – do come, if you're not busy. He's in oxygen, and he's my best friend.'

'We're not busy. Thanks, Alison.'

'What an amazing woman,' Sue said later. 'Do you think she was trying to tell us she was Nkrumah's mistress?'

'I don't believe Alison would try to tell anyone anything. She either tells you or she doesn't, so we shall never know for sure.'

*

'It's not what you promised me at all, Johnny. It's nothing but parties, picnics and balls,' Sue moaned in ecstasy as we luxuriated by Michael's pool, awaiting our host, who had gone to fetch his other guests.

'Savour it while it lasts.'

'I do. I do! But we have two more days before "The Crunch",' which is what we had dubbed the start of our up-country tour after the Freetown bonanza, 'so I refuse to think about it yet.'

'I thought you were looking forward to it?'

'Of course I am. It's what we're here for. But you must admit this is all pretty seductive.'

She waved a hand round the gardens, perched above the rocks at the edge of the sea. A sprinkler was flinging a coiled necklace of diamonds over the emerald grass and the perfume of frangipani hung in the air like incense. Two tame gazelles grazed under the tree, nibbling the fallen blossoms and flicking their stumpy tails.

'It could be worse.'

Michael was an extremely prosperous young businessman with the dubious distinction of owning both a Mercedes *and* a Range Rover. He employed a staff of six to run his luxurious establishment and a private zoo housing a motley assortment of indigenous small mammals and birds, and some fat rabbits for the table. He was extremely popular, for he was bluff and handsome and as yet unattached.

A walking zebra-crossing approached from the house, the dense black of his skin intersected by the gleaming white of his shoes and socks and shorts and shirt and his face-splitting smile. He asked us if we would like something to drink as if it was the funniest idea he'd ever had. He must be new, I thought. The stewards we'd met so far had all been suaver than Sean Connery.

'Sue?'

'Oh...beer, I think.'

'Two beers, thank you.'

'Alan says we can have Arthur and the car tomorrow to visit some of the beaches.'

'Great! We can take a picnic.'

'May's arranged all that.' May was Alan's vivacious other half, with a gift for chatter and a genius for generosity. 'I couldn't stop her. She's packing their ice-box with beer and soft-drinks. They've got a beach umbrella, folding chairs and everything. The car, all loaded, will pick us up at ten, and Arthur will take us wherever we want. He knows the coast like the back of his hand.'

'How can we ever return their hospitality?'

'If we get back alive, we can take them out to dinner. What else can we do?'

'They have hospitality the way Mrs Olive has minor ailments. No sooner over one bout than they're struck down with another.'

'P'raps it's seasonal, and during the rainy season it all sinks without trace.'

'We'd better have an early night tomorrow. It's going to be a gruelling drive – into the unknown.'

'You make it sound like "Startrek". Let's have dinner, just the two of us, at The Atlantic Beach. I hear it's special.'

Michael arrived with the rest of his guests, a party of eight which included three women we had not met.

'Alison you already know, and the rest are all Mays,' he said.

'What do you mean?'

'This is May, and this is May and this is May and that's May.'

'How incredible! Four Sue's I could believe. But May is a fairly unusual name.'

'Oh, we're used to the jokes, Sue,' said one of the Mays. 'It's a small British community here, so we're often all together.'

' "Here we have four Mays," ' said Alan's May, ' "but the fifth certainly will!" '

They all four nodded their heads and looked resigned.

For lunch we had groundnut stew with plantains, and we drank chilled Chablis from silver goblets. The pudding had just arrived when there was a twittering screech, and two furry shapes flashed across the lawn, sliced through the herbaceous border and dived under the table. A May screamed, and several others jumped up and started running.

'It's only Mowgli and Rikki-Tikki!' Michael shouted after the fleeing Mays. 'They're tame. They won't bite!' Sue, as unobtrusively as possible, climbed onto the sideboard pulling her dress tight round her ankles.

'Hyacinth!'

The laughing steward came running. With a name like that no wonder the world seems risible.

'You go get de basket for de small beef. Dey make plenty humbug. An' go swipe two eggs from de kitchen and bringem chop

chop. After, you go fix de fence good, so de beef no make humbug.'

Since the luncheon party had disintegrated, we deployed ourselves round the garden to watch the ensuing chase. The mongeese scooted across the lawn squeaking with glee, driving the gazelles ahead of them at a dignified high-heeled trot. When they found the sprinkler they turned somersaults and splashed about in the damp grass, pushing their snouts blissfully up into the cool jet and washing behind their ears.

Hyacinth emerged from the house with a large basket and two eggs. Donning a pair of stout gardening gloves (so much for

'They're tame!'), Michael approached the water-sports making reassuring noises.

The animals paused and looked up, their beady little eyes alight with expectation. Spying the eggs in Michael's hand, they began to chatter with excitement, leaping about, and standing on their hind legs impatiently scrabbling at the air. When he put the eggs gently on the grass, one started to play football, dribbling his egg round in little circles, while the other turned on his back and juggled adroitly with all four feet. The juggler was the first to break his shell, covering his tummy in goo. While he was preoccupied with getting his greedy nose into the sticky yoke, Michael grabbed him, and put him amid outraged squeals of protest into the basket and shut the lid. The same procedure was efficacious for the footballer, though he had to have help to break his 'ball'.

'Sorry about that.' Michael was beaming and covered in sweat after his exertions. 'The little buggers are always getting out. I think we must have some champagne with the fruit salad.'

'What it is to be in Oxygen,' Sue said, visibly brightening.

'Hyacinth!'

'Is that *really* his name?'

'Oh, yes. Christened and all. He has a brother called Flobert and a sister called Menthol, but she disappeared when she was two.'

'How do you mean, "disappeared"?'

'She disappeared! About six years ago. It's not unheard of. She was probably given to one of the Secret Societies.'

'I don't understand any of this.'

'Cannibalism.'

'I don't believe it.'

'Oh, it's much less common than it used to be. One of the present Government's boasts is that they've stamped it out. But these practices have been going on for years, and when you're dealing with superstition and ju-ju, mere penalties won't stop them.'

'You mean they eat flesh for good magic?'

'Yes. Power, potency, success and so on. Nobody outside knows much about the Secret Societies, mind you, beyond the titles. "The Baboon", "The Leopard" and so forth. But rumours abound of dreadful rites. And cannibalism still goes on, though nobody likes to talk about it. It's often children that vanish without trace. If a mother, for example, gives her child to the Society, then no one is going to make a fuss if *she* doesn't complain.'

'Mothers give their *own children*?'

'Sometimes. Life and death mean something different out here. The infant mortality rate is difficult to establish accurately, but they reckon it's still over fifty per cent. What is the loss of one more child if it's given as a sacrifice and will bring all that good ju-ju?'

'Oh my God.'

'Only a few months ago, my foreman heard his steward quarrelling bitterly with his wife in the kitchen. When he asked them the cause of the argument, the steward said that his wife had given one of their daughters to the Society. My foreman was appalled, as you can imagine. But the steward's principal grievance, apparently, was not that his daughter had been given to be killed, but *that he hadn't been consulted about it first.*'

'What is the Government doing about it?'

'The crime is called "Dealing in Persons", and it carries the death penalty, of course, *if* it's discovered. Last year, a cabinet minister was hanged for it. They couldn't hush *that* case up. They found the body of a child with vital organs missing in his deep freeze.'

※

With Alison's story of 'the coup' still fresh in our minds, when we arrived at The Atlantic Beach we were convinced we had landed in the middle of an armed insurrection. Thirty policemen bristling with rifles and bulging with holsters lined the steps to the entrance, and from the shrubbery and the palm-thickets that fringed the beach came the rustle of innumerable heavy feet.

'What's happening?' I asked one of the less encumbered and more senior-looking officers.

'The Royal Princess Farah Shahbanou of Iran is happening, sir,' he said, 'all over Sierra Leone.'

We had seen posters in town bearing her photograph, and had gathered that she was paying a state visit.

'And now she's happening at The Atlantic Beach.'

'Has she arrived yet?'

'Any minute now, madam. Pay no attention to us. We're only here to ensure there's no trouble. Have a good dinner, sir, madam.'

The tables were laid out on a tiled terrace, level with the beach which was floodlit, so that at first the reflection from the blazing white sand almost hurt one's eyes. The waves were breaking just beyond where the darkness began again, and the surf snaked and flounced in the artificial light like a phosphorescent feather-boa being wafted by an invisible coquette. A huge crab glinted green for a moment as it wobbled towards the rocks. The perennial cloud above had thinned, so that a mass of unfamiliar stars peeped through then faded shyly.

A small group of musicians played old-fashioned 'pop' at a level that did not preclude conversation... 'Fee-lings, Ow-Wow-Wow Fee-lings...'

'I had an aunt by marriage who was a missionary in Tibet,' I said, scanning the menu. 'A wiry little spinster with freckles and a wet kiss. She had met the Dalai Lama and drunk tea with rancid butter in it. When I was about eight, I hid a lump of butter among my socks for a month. It got covered in fluff but I put it in my tea. It didn't make me sick, so I was convinced I had the stamina to brave strange lands and convert the heathen. I can't recall exactly when I went off God, but my taste for travel began with a greasy cup of tea.'

'Travel for me was standing in a long frock at the rail of a big white ship with the wind in my hair, listening to the music of temple-dancers from a golden pagoda, and having a dozen porters to carry my luggage.'

The shrubbery began to heave as black faces poked through the evergreen to catch a glimpse of the Princess Farah Shahbanoo and her companions as they bore down upon us. The head-waiter was in a panic.

'The princess's party is bigger than we expected, sir,' he hissed, his eyes showing an arc of white above the irises. 'They would like to sit on the terrace, and we don't have the tables. Would you mind sitting inside? I'm so sorry to ask you...'

How could two mere Thespians disrupt a state visit? The princess herself saw the situation, and was most polite and apologetic.

As our photographs had appeared in the same newspaper as hers had on the day of her arrival, with a little nudging from Sue she deduced who we were, and perhaps thinking that we might leaven the dough of a formal occasion she cordially invited us to join her party.

It is one of the advantages of being an actor that one is persona grata among all classes of society. This is not surprising at the top of the ladder, since, without apology, I find my colleagues with few exceptions to be intelligent, warm and amusing, with a greater ability to communicate than most, and an interest in others, perhaps because of our work, which is genuine and unforced and spans the whole social scale. But what is more surprising is that we are equally accepted by the so-called 'scum of the earth'. Many years ago, when I worked at the Citizens' Theatre in Glasgow, which was then in the heart of the old Gorbals, considered to be the worst slum in Europe, a razor-gang of desperate youths and their pinched-faced girl-friends, called 'Herries', used to hang about our stage-door. They enjoyed chatting with us as we went in for the evening performance, and frequently offered to escort solitary actresses through the dangerous streets after the show. During this period, one of their number was 'sent away' for five years for attempting to kill a member of a rival gang. They were not 'fans'. They never came to see a show, except occasionally our Christmas pantomime when we managed to wheedle free tickets. They did not consider us glamorous. Perhaps they thought of us as misfits like themselves. We 'played' for a living. We did it at night. We were relatively poor, dressed in jeans and not suits, and we did not reject them or preach, though we certainly did not condone their violence. We were accepted as equals and cherished as confederates.

Dancing on the crowded floor later, I whispered to Sue, 'Africa might turn out to be short on golden pagodas, but I bet you didn't expect an Arabian princess.'

'I'm afraid I'm going to wake up in a minute and find that it's pissing outside and I've got to go to the launderette.'

'Don't worry, we'll both wake up tomorrow all right.' It was the start of our tour up-country. 'At six-thirty to be precise.'

'How many lumps do you take in your greasy tea?'

Chapter Two

The Crunch

The Land Rover, laden with plastic water-containers, tins of food, camp beds, mosquito nets, and an ominously large first-aid kit, drew up at last in front of the headmaster's office in Bo. The four-hour drive had left us parched and rattled and covered with fine red dust, but what a feast for the eyes. Populous mud villages, with life strung out like a tapestry along the edge of the road. Humble stalls and sprawling markets and sleek little goats climbing over piles of rubbish, while scrawny hens scratched busily among their chicks. Banana plantations and oil-palms and termite hills the shape of six-foot phallic mushrooms. In every dark verandah, a leg or an arm was draped over the side of a gently swinging hammock; at every bridge and bend in the road, the wreck of a car or a truck told a salutary story.

We stopped only once at a shabby 'routier', ostensibly to drink coca-cola, though a higher priority after our early start was to find a lavatory. Sue was directed through a door to the back yard, from whence she returned after an unlikely ten-second interval with a look of alarm on her face. We had had little expectation of finding Kleenex coming out of the wall, or fragrant 'Blue Flush' in the pan, and were grateful, simply, to have found somewhere out of sight of the passing traffic.

'What's the problem?' I asked irritably. 'It may not be the Dorchester, pet, but our need is pressing.'

'The place is two feet square, and there are three huge dogs asleep in there. Would you like to go first?'

The dogs, which were in fact quite small and mangy, were lying in a motionless heap all round the pan for coolness. Quashing morbid thoughts of dying in agony demented and ranting with foam-flecked lips, I nudged them tentatively with my desert boot. They were as reluctant to wake up as I was to wake them, and I'm ashamed to confess that I had to call the owner, who lifted them by their flea-bitten necks and flung them, uncomplaining, out into the baking sun.

The procedure at all the schools we visited was roughly the same. Hot and dishevelled, we were ushered into the headmaster's office and cordially welcomed. Chairs were brought, and while we sat opposite his desk steaming and passing swollen tongues over cracked lips, teachers and heads of departments and other interested parties arrived to pay their respects. The venue was discussed in detail, frequently offering us a choice of two halls, with names like Ugabugwa or Mbwmbwmwe, neither of which, of course, had we set eyes upon; we were therefore at a disadvantage when consulted about our preference. Refreshments were sometimes provided in the form of tea or scraped oranges to suck, which we fell upon with unseemly voracity. After a long journey, our enthusiasm for social intercourse was not high, and we should have liked to say, 'Let's see the hall, dump our bags wherever we're staying, wash if there's water, have something to eat and get on with it.' On our trip, this ritual took place twice a day. For them, it happened perhaps once in a lifetime, so we had to exercise tact, which once we were ensconced was not so difficult as might be supposed, for the African face (at the risk of generalising), perhaps due to the generosity of the mouth and the prominence that the colour of the skin gives to the eyes, is singularly expressive, so that concern and pleasure play across it without guile or hypocrisy.

'You will be guests of the Government while you're here, Mr Fraser, Miss Farmer.' It was impossible not to be touched by his eagerness to please. 'We have arranged accommodation for you at the Government Rest House. I hope it will be to your satisfaction.'

Checkmate. As guests of the Government we were obliged to smile at our plight. The Rest House was composed of a series of little bungalows set among gums and acacias in a dusty glade, which may sound charming, but three months of unremitting downpour during the rainy season make it impossible to keep the outside of buildings pristine and neat. The red mud bounces up the wall, and the deluge washes off whatever paint or distemper they use in the first year, giving even newly built premises an air of dilapidation.

Inside, the concrete floor was scattered with the remnants of dead cockroaches. The softboard ceiling, torn and rotted in parts, gave onto dark caverns where nameless horrors waited to pounce. One of the two rickety iron beds had a single sheet covering the stains on the mouldy mattress, and was crowned with a knotted flourish of tattered grey mosquito netting. There was wiring of a sort, but not a bulb to be seen. (Our driver explained that the current is liable to surge, so that bulbs left in sockets tend to blow out.) A rusty tin can, a pungent loo without water, and a squalid bathroom containing two buckets of what looked like thick lentil soup completed our amenities.

The old retainer was padding off on dusty bare feet to show me to my bungalow when Sue grabbed my arm.

'Let's share!' she said. 'It's not that I'm scared or anything. It's just that I'm going home unless you do.'

'There's no sheet.'

'You can have mine – and there's a net in the Land Rover.'

But we each got a single sheet, we rigged up a second net, and Arthur, our driver, bought some bulbs at the local market. We reserved the lentil soup for the loo, rejecting Sue's unsupported contention that liver flukes can jump up and bite you on the bottom, and we unloaded a container of clean water from the supply we had brought with us.

I was unpacking the insecticide when a piercing cackle emanated from the pungent end of the house.

'She can't have lost her sanity already,' I thought, running to the rescue.

Sue was standing stark naked in the bathroom, throwing fresh water at herself with manic glee, using the rusty tin can as a calabash.

'It's lovely!' she squealed, and cackled again like one of the

witches in the parts of *Macbeth* that we didn't do. 'Come on in!'
So I did, and we splashed each other and sloshed about in the
lovely stuff like children having their first paddle. We were dis-
proportionately euphoric at thus adapting to our up-country
environment.

❋

The Traveller was the only establishment of its kind that we
passed on our way to the school. It may, I hope, be the only

establishment of its kind, period. It looked neither interesting ethnically, nor inviting in a European way, but as our appetites had been sharpened by our bath-time hysteria we asked Arthur to stop.

The entrance was draped with a banner proclaiming 'Night Club and Restaurant where you meet All the Best People', and underneath on the lintel of the door was carved a motto which gave us many hours of fruitless speculation: 'Man Must Wack.' There were no people to meet however, of quality or otherwise, though a dozen tables covered in oil-cloth bearing crusted bottles of sauce and plastic condiment-sets, and a pervasive smell of burnt fat, suggested that customers had either recently departed or were expected.

An old man in a once-white monkey-jacket emerged from a doorway, and on seeing us his face became a mask of dismay. He held out his pink palms and shook his jowls.

'No chop!' he lamented. But when we shrugged and made to leave, he relented, and propelled us physically to a table mouthing a speech that only Arthur understood.

'Meat pancake,' Arthur translated. 'That's it.'

Arthur had declined our invitation to join us, for he was staying with relatives and was expected for a mid-day meal. This inter-dependence among relations is typically African, and each family network appears to cover the continent. It is the one factor that puts the biggest strain on mixed marriages, for when you marry an individual you take on the family as well. If you emigrate to the moon, they will find you there and come to keep you company – lots of them, sometimes, and for as long as they care to stay. It cuts both ways of course, and by marriage you inherit prospective hosts across the country in a chain more extensive than The Holiday Inns.

'Meat pancake's fine,' I said.

As the aroma from the kitchen did not make our mouths water, Sue asked, 'Any eggs?'

The waiter scuttled away and returned holding up one apologetic finger.

'That'll do,' she said with finality, and though the resulting omelette was the size of a wet lady's handkerchief, she could not be persuaded to sample my pancake, which was filled with what tasted like very old mangy dog.

During the repast, three young men tottered across the threshold in a state of intoxication. They noisily ordered Guinness, which is locally brewed and bears no resemblance except in colour to the stuff that is good for you. On seeing two flushed white faces in this remote eating-spot, they rolled towards us and affably shook us by the hand. Collapsing at the table next to ours, they produced a portable radio which was unique in my experience, in that it was capable of playing all the stations at once, and at a volume altogether surprising in so small an instrument.

By the time we had finished our meal Sue's hand was clamped to her good ear. When I could see her face (for she kept ducking under the table between mouthfuls, as an ugly bug with horns and a black floating train dive-bombed us unmercifully throughout), her brows were knotted and beaded with sweat.

'Let's move outside.' I motioned to a covered porch with some easy chairs which was adjacent to the dining-room. 'We'll get a breeze from the window, and we can relax for half an hour before the performance.'

We had no sooner settled in the welcome draught than the screeching transistor snapped off, and the three young men appeared at our side in a silent menacing group.

'We're not good enough for you, man, is that it?'

Too late, I realised we had offended them.

'Why did you move away?'

'We're not used to the heat, and we wanted some air, that's all,' I explained.

'You don't like our music!' Another one pushed forward. 'We played it for *you*, man, that's why we played it.'

'Thank you. I appreciate it. But I've told you, we've just arrived from England, and the heat is killing us. We wanted to be near the window.'

'O.K.' The ringleader seemed mollified, and held out his hand. We had already gone through the elaborate ritual of greeting, which in West Africa consists of the usual handclasp, progressing to a closer grip above the thumb, and ending with both parties sliding their palms apart with a cool snap of the fingers. It is a much more eloquent avowal of friendship than the perfunctory 'how-de-do' practised in Europe. Thinking the misunderstanding cleared up, as I held a cigarette in my right hand I held up my left to shake his. He bashed it aside in a resurgence of incomprehensible aggression. I discovered later that the left hand is associated with weakness and inferiority, and my offering it to him was like a calculated insult.

Incensed by my blunder he raised his voice.

'Show me your papers! What are you doing in our country anyway? You show me your papers. We don't need you here.'

The man was not a policeman. The law would doubtless have been on my side had I refused to comply with his request. My sole reason for instantly producing my passport was grovelling cowardice. There were three of them and two of us, and we were a long way from home.

The others crowded round, snatching it from hand to hand, spilling my shopping-list of jabs onto the beer-slopped floor.

He shouted something unintelligible at Sue.

'Sorry?' she said, and he shouted again. I couldn't understand him.

'Is he speaking English?' Sue muttered to me.

'You think I don't speak English?' Now we understood him, and the mounting anger in his tone, only too well. 'I speak English!' He counted on his fingers. 'I speak Limba, Temne, Krio, English – Parlez-vous Français?' he asked in a surprisingly good accent.

'Oui.'

We embarked on a conversation in French, during which we explained the object of our visit to Sierra Leone. He translated into Krio for his friends as he went along, and they subsided into a silence more of disbelief, I fear, than respect. Once again our 'vagabond' image broke down the barriers, but above all the demonstration of his linguistic skill saved the day.

I never drink alcohol before a show. I am not fond of Irish Guinness, and I loathe the African brew. But there are times when such considerations are over-ridden by the instinct for self-preservation, and by the time Arthur arrived to take us to the school we all had our arms around each other and I was knocking the filthy stuff back like an Irish navvy.

*

The hall was packed with boys and girls in spotless uniforms, electric blue and white and red and orange. There were no fans, and what air might have circulated was effectively blocked at each open window by a squirming wall of children considered too young for our cultural fare. Their mouths and eyes were wide with astonishment as we strode onto the stage in our strange clothes. Before we even started I could feel my boots filling up, as the sweat trickled from the crown of my head, forming little tributaries under my clammy shirt to join the streams that meandered subterraneously down through my nylon tights.

A big black Sister, with a bosom more like that of an Earth Mother than a Bride of Christ, could not be restrained from delivering an introductory speech. She held our biographies in one hand, but disdained to consult them.

'This afternoon, boys and girls, ladies and gentlemen, we are having the privilege of seeing in our midst two distinguished dramatists from England – Mr John Farmer and Miss Suzan Fraser. Miss Fraser is famous all over for the films that she has been making, and in particular she is noted for playing the famous part of Dracula in *The Prince of Darkness*. Furthermore, she was winning the prizes of the Savoy Theatre for her interpretations, because Lord George Knew Her Father. Mr Farmer is also famous for his big parts. He has been playing with Suzan Fraser before this date, and he is distinguished for playing the big part of Romeo in *Hamlet* at Stratford-upon-Shakespeare.'

The children in the provinces were a total joy to play to. Less sophisticated than the city children, their reactions were spontaneous and voluble, their silences rapt. When they were studying the plays, they would often speak the immortal lines along with us, their eyes shining. 'The quality of mercy...', 'Tomorrow and tomorrow...' When I jumped at seeing Banquo's ghost, they jumped too, and yelped with excitement.

> I have given suck, and know
> How tender 'tis to love the babe that milks me:

> I would, while it was smiling in my face,
> Have plucked my nipple from his boneless gums
> And dashed the brains out, had I so sworn as you
> Have done to this.

Their eyes were troubled pools. They shook their heads and gave little moans and held onto their neighbours in the extremity of their concern.

> I dare do all that may become a man.
> Who dares do more, is none.

They grunted and nodded wisely, and muttered, 'How true! How true!'

I have never felt a more vital rapport with any audience than I did with these children throughout West Africa. Playing to the Elizabethan groundlings must have been like this, though certainly not more rewarding.

✻

Our Rest House after dark was alive with entomological interest. Spiders like catherine-wheels, and fluffy beige moths and sneaky little mosquitoes which hardly buzz at all (they just give you malaria), and a thriving colony of large ginger cockroaches which were always in a hurry. They hurtled about like clockwork frankfurters. I managed by careful 'aiming off' to crunch a few underfoot, mainly to placate Sue (for I knew I was a helpless Canute commanding the waves), who was tightly tucked inside her mosquito net patiently whimpering, and alternately squirting insecticide and stitching the bigger holes with trembling fingers. During the night Sue rose to attend to the lentil soup, and the beam from her torch revealed an army of ants swarming over the squashed cockroaches. In the morning, nothing remained of them but a few tattered scales.

✻

After a long drive and two performances, the Volunteer's bungalow where we spent the following night seemed like Claridge's. There were three light bulbs, a delicious smell of curry from the kitchen, and a trickle of water in the bathroom tap. Just cold to be sure, but it was wet and almost clear and it was sufficient to work up a sticky lather, though it required some patience to rinse it off. Sue grabbed the opportunity to wash our drip-dry costumes, and was hanging them out on the porch when Jill, our hostess, intervened. It is possible to dry clothes outside in this part of Africa only if they are pressed thoroughly afterwards with a very hot iron, for there is a bug called 'the tumble fly' which lays its eggs in the damp seams. The eggs hatch into maggots on contact with the skin, and they burrow beneath the surface growing fat and causing 'boils'. The only way to remove them is to close the opening they make on the way in with vaseline, which cuts off the supply of air. They then come to the surface, and can be popped out like a stone from a cherry. Sue needed no coaxing to bring the dripping costumes indoors. We were regaled with stories of rhinoceros beetles the size of mice that fly, lethal snakes and scorpions and bugs that go for the eyes. Jill's school had to close for a week when there was an epidemic. After such gruesome tales I anticipated a restless night, and I was right for the wrong reasons.

Jill was a typical Volunteer (Voluntary Services Overseas). An ordinary youngster doing an extraordinary job. A V.S.O. of twenty we met later in a remote village had been stoned and seriously hurt. Another had gone without food or water for three days when his motor-bike broke down in the desert. We met many, and all were full of courage and enthusiasm and short of money. Though their accommodation is sometimes princely by comparison with the poorer Africans', their furnishings are sparse and the luxuries non-existent. Yet they were all glad to share what little they had with us.

There was one spare bed for Sue and an empty room for myself and Arthur, who, incredible as it seemed, had no blood-ties or acquaintances to host him during his stay in Magburoka. We brought the camp-beds from the Land Rover, fitted them up, and lit an anti-mosquito spiral since we were too lazy to fix up the nets. These spirals burn slowly throughout the night giving off acrid smoke, which seems to deter mosquitoes but certainly induces dreams of the house being on fire. But I was to be denied dreams of any sort, for Arthur was a noisy sleeper.

His snoring was distinguished by its variety and richness. It was like a sixty-piece orchestra. The long in-breaths rose from a terrible base rattle pregnant with the threat of danger, interrupted by a series of unexpected snorts like muffled grenades exploding, to a Wagnerian climax with a mighty roll on the timpani and a clash of cymbals. Then followed the out-breath, which was a modulated moan of release, accompanied by a flapping of the lips like ripples lapping on the side of a boat. This pattern of sound was also part of a larger pattern, wave upon wave, which ended in such a stentorian storm in the nasal and bronchial passages that nature demanded a short period of respite before starting on the next onslaught. During this pause, however, there was no peace, for Arthur also ground his teeth. The same cavities which gave his snoring such resonance amplified this little idiosyncrasy to a volume consistent with the sound of a prisoner sawing through his bars. At that time Arthur also suffered from nightmares, for twice during that endless night he gave a low moan, which rose slowly, tantalisingly, in pitch till it suddenly ended abruptly with a very loud shout.

As the sky outside our window finally grew pale with the coming day he started to fart, so I went for a walk.

*

The performance in the morning was cool and pleasant. The children had garlanded the stage with hibiscus and bougainvillea, and the blackboard was illustrated with scenes from a savagely African Venice. They had never seen actors before. One teacher confided that a pupil had approached her afterwards, disillusion dawning in his eyes. 'Do you mean to tell me that when I go to see a cowboy film, those people aren't *really* cowboys?'

We drove eighty miles to the next school on a laterite road that was fairly smooth, although dusty. I had mastered the art of absorbing the bumps by sitting forward in the back seat of the Land Rover and concentrating, so that I could anticipate the holes in the road. Arthur stopped in a village to collect a puppy for one of his sons, a scruffy, docile little creature that piddled in Sue's Balthazar hat, and a wicker-cage containing two grey doves flecked with peacock-blue. They had white breasts, long, slender beaks, and eyes like black stars. The urchin, or 'bo-bo', who sold them, had snared them with a bent stick and a loop of liana. How they survived that journey without water I shall never know, but they did. They were a present for the relatives that Arthur would be snoring with that night.

As the platform they had constructed at our second school was six feet high, and the only means of access to it was either by scaling it like a cliff, or doing it in stages with the help of a wobbly chair, we asked if there were any steps we could use. They were penitent, and shook their heads, so we agreed that we would manage somehow. In the time it took us to snatch a bite to eat and don our costumes, however, the boys had knocked up a very serviceable flight of stairs.

Afterwards, in the headmaster's office, we sat in a large circle while the teachers introduced themselves one by one. They stood, announcing their names, the schools they represented, the subjects they taught, and how many miles their pupils had travelled. On this occasion, which was not unusual, the pupils from an outlying district had overcome the problem of chronic lack of transport by clubbing together to pay for a truck and the petrol to bring them seventy-five miles over MAMBA roads (Miles And Miles of Bugger All), driving all day in the crucifying heat, with a five-hour journey back in the dark.

The teachers were invited by the head to comment on our performance, though the guidelines he laid down were narrow, being somewhat prejudiced in our favour.

'Perhaps you would like to tell Mr Fraser and Miss Farmer what thrilled you most about their presentation.'

It reminded me of the story of Sam Goldwyn showing one of his films for the first time to a friend. 'I want you to be honest,' he said. 'Don't spare my feelings. I want to know if you think it's the best film ever made, or is it only a masterpiece.'

There were two white teachers among the group of twenty or so. I was often struck by how unhealthy Europeans look in black company. Our bodies seem flaccid and our skins show blemishes and our hair looks lank. But Odela eclipsed black and white alike. She was a liberated intellectual, elegantly gowned in kingfisher-blue with a matching bandanna, and she glowed. She was gentle and assured and more beautiful than a black Nefertiti.

To meet these lovely, shy, laughing people, and above all the children, made up a hundred-fold for all the discomfort.

In the evening Odela invited us to 'chop', in this case a succulent stew containing both meat and fish 'in palaver' which we ate with our fingers, kneading our mealey-meal into a rubbery ball and scooping the stew from a communal dish. Sue hated it, but the occasion was a fitting celebration for our last evening 'up-country'.

Arthur had delivered his doves. Since our Rest House was little better than the first, and we were expected as guests in Michael's house overlooking the bay, he offered to drive through the night back to Freetown.

The stalls along the road were aglow with night-lights. The balmy air carried the smell of wood-smoke and cooking and dung and oranges, and the spicy, dry tang of the parched earth.

I leant forward to Sue, who was in the front seat.

'Well, we've survived "the Crunch", pet. Sorry you came?'

I had to say it twice, as I had popped it into the wrong ear.

'I wouldn't have missed it for a twenty-part serial with lots of repeats.'

*

After breakfast of pink grapefruit, sausages, bacon, scrambled eggs, baked-beans, toast and honey, we set off for York Bay, a sizzling paradise, with fishermen dragging their coracles over the black beach on rollers of felled-pine, the young boys naked and dusted with sand. In the shade of a giant conifer, a mixed group sat mending their nets singing songs of melancholy beauty and refusing to be photographed. It was nothing to do with any fear that their 'soul' might be taken away. I respected their reticence. For they resented any suggestion of 'tourists' taking pictures of 'monkeys at the zoo'.

We sat in a thatched shack drinking coca-cola and dipping from time to time in the near-boiling sea. Sue cut her foot on a rock, and I disinfected it with rum (now, it's out!), since, in this climate, wounds go green and fester within the hour.

It was not surprising that in the evening we felt a little weak (four hours of combined sauna and hot-bath are not invigorating), but we diligently bedecked ourselves in our finery for a television interview which had been arranged for us the previous week, and made our way to the studio. Personal publicity is of no interest to Sue or myself unless it helps to promote 'the show'. Since we were leaving Sierra Leone the next day, our reason for accepting the invitation to appear on the programme was ambassadorial, rather than promotional. Diplomacy is almost as important an aspect in a tour of this kind as education. It was therefore extremely galling to find that, having devoted our last evening in this beautiful country to duty, our interviewer had not only pissed off to cover some more urgent event, but had omitted to advise us that the interview was cancelled. This kind of unreliable behaviour is common among Africans, and though it can be profoundly frustrating for punctilious Northerners, one quickly learns to shrug it off and change one's plans.

We had invited Alan and May and Michael and Alison and some other friends to join us for a late supper. Finding ourselves free at seven-thirty and dressed for the opera, we had the choice of waiting at the restaurant with the risk of getting bored or tipsy, or seeking out an adventure.

On our way to the studio, our attention had been drawn to a noisy crowd in a brightly lit courtyard. Arthur had explained that a cock-fight was in progress, and though we disapproved in principle of such a barbaric sport I was nevertheless keen to see it for myself. Sue took some persuading, not least because of our incongruous dress, but she finally agreed.

The cock-pit was a series of benches arranged in tiers round a circle about ten feet across. It was strip-lit from above, and the benches were full of men in a state of vociferous excitement. Our arrival caused a considerable stir, but the laying of bets was in full swing, and after making room for us on one of the upper levels only the children continued to gaze at us while the adults returned their attention to the cocks in the ring.

In the shadowy periphery, proud owners held their birds in one hand ruffling their plumage, and cooling them with a fine mist of water from their mouths, which they spat out in a long raspberry. The neck and leg-feathers had been cropped to reveal the strong muscles under the naked skin. The men taped steel spurs over the existing dew-claws and squeezed lime on the glinting metal, partly to disinfect the wounds they would cause, and partly to sting their opponents. Each bird was weighed in hand-held scales and matched for the ensuing contests. Afterwards their scars were lovingly washed in basins of water, while scarlet combs quivered over glittering, indignant eyes.

At the start of a fight, the cocks are placed under cages like meat fly-covers, at opposite sides of the pit. The betting becomes frantic, while money is passed in bundles to men with improvised blackboards in the front row. As the shouting and tick-tack messages reach a climax, a bell is rung, the covers are lifted, and the cockerels are face to face. In a flurry of feathers they fly at each other, claws slashing, each trying to trample the other underfoot. Without the metal spurs a fighting cock could injure his opponent and bring him to submission, but with the addition of these miniature scythes they inflict severe damage on one another, and despite the value to their owners of these champions, death, though not invariably the outcome, is quite usual.

In spite of the cruelty of this spectacle, the gleam in the eyes of the spectators was not blood-lust. Like many poor agrarian people, they are indifferent to the suffering of animals. It was simply gambling-fever, no different from the hysteria of the race-course or the greyhound-track. I could never condone cock-fighting as a sport, but I am ashamed to admit that when we had put a couple of Leones on a splendid black bird with thighs like Nureyev, we shouted along with the rest.

Our dinner guests, who were seeing a colleague off at the airport, would have been unable to watch our television interview had we done one, so it was Sue's idea to play a joke.

When Alan and May and the others arrived at the restaurant we greeted them with long faces.

'How did it go?' Alan asked anxiously.

We both shook our heads and cast our eyes to the ground.

'What happened?' He was beginning to look alarmed.

'It was my fault,' Sue said. 'I'm so sorry, Alan. I'm afraid we've dropped you right in it. But the interviewer goaded us so dreadfully! "What do you think you're doing in our country anyway? Bringing Shakespeare to Africa! What's Shakespeare got to do with us?" and things like that.'

'What did you say?'

'Well, I'm afraid I might have been a bit indiscreet. I just said the British Council had more money than sense, and that the whole thing had been atrociously organised anyway, that it was shovelling good money down the drain, bringing us all the way to this stinking, rotten country, just to play to a few grotty school-kids and a bunch of cannibals.'

Alan felt for the back of a chair, while the others gathered round speechless with horror.

'Jesus Christ!' he said, going ashen.

Alan was the gentlest and most conscientious of men and I couldn't keep the pretence up much longer.

'Don't worry, Alan,' Sue said. 'I'll take full responsibility.'

'No, no. It's just as much my fault,' I said. 'We were on the air, after all. I should never have taken a swipe at him and called him a Dirty Black Bastard.'

This broke our credibility. Everybody shouted in derision, and Alan let out a long 'Phew!' and punched me playfully in the chest.

'You wee buggers!' he said, and Sue leapt into his arms giggling and kissing him better, but it took him a couple of stiff whiskies before he could enjoy the joke.

At the end of a perfect evening, the bill always appears less daunting than it does in retrospect the following morning when you wish you had drunk less and checked it. But even through our vinous haze that bill seemed exorbitant. I have always found it embarrassing, especially when wishing to appear unconcerned about the mere price of returning lavish hospitality, to pore over a list of indecipherable items and figures counting on one's fingers and anxiously shaking one's head. With sinking heart I held a muttered conversation with Sue, while Alan politely asked if he might order some more coffee and French cognac all round.

'Of course!' What else could I say?

I cornered the head waiter and ascertained that travellers' cheques would be acceptable. Between us, Sue and I ripped out fistfuls from our living allowance for the next six weeks, determined to postpone till the morning all thought of what emergency measures we should have to take to replenish our resources. We were signing away like Donny Osmond at his fan-club when the mirth among our guests became too uproarious to ignore.

'That'll teach you to pull my leg!' Alan gasped, wiping the tears from his eyes. 'The last laugh's on you!' He had already paid the bill, which amounted, he assured us, to less than a quarter of the spurious one that he had arranged for us to be given, and he refused with the threat of losing his friendship to accept repayment. 'You can stand us the brandy, John. It's been a pleasure having you. Bon voyage, and come back soon.'

Sue squeezed my hand till the knuckles cracked.

I said nothing, for I had a lump in my throat.

＊

To reach the airport from Freetown, one has to cross the Rokel River Estuary by ferry. Michael and Alison and Alan and May stood waving on the quay as we left the Land Rover in the hold, and climbed up with Arthur to the passenger deck. Leaving across water is so melancholy and final. The vista of departure; the widening emptiness in between. When we could no longer see each other's eyes, tears crept into ours, not just for the friends waving goodbye on the distant bank, but for the teachers and the Volunteers and the thousands of children who had transformed an arduous task into a labour of love.

Chapter Three

The Jungle

Many expatriates we met like Lagos. To the Nigerians, it has the magic of the capital. It is bustling and raunchy, with all the affluence and poverty and amenities and flesh-pots of a big city. It is nevertheless called by some the arsehole of the world, and Ibadan (which was on our itinerary) is said to be a hundred miles up it. This latter allegation I found to be unjust, though I never grew to tolerate Lagos.

I should dearly like to visit Nigeria again. If my ensuing observations seem jaundiced and unkind, I hope they will be counteracted by my account of our experiences later throughout this fascinating country. My loathing is reserved purely for Lagos.

The climate is debilitating. Only seven degrees north of the Equator, the combination of humidity and air-pollution is oppressive. The discovery of oil, and the subsequent love affair with the internal-combustion engine, has brought the city to a standstill. The average speed of a motor-vehicle at almost any time of the day in this city-wide traffic-jam is one mile an hour, and the honking and swerving and jostling for position tear one's nerves to tatters. The poor wash their dishes in the open sewers – sluggish trickles by the roadside – and it is said that they have built up an immunity to cholera by eating the rats. Organic refuse, such as one sees in other overcrowded cities like Calcutta or Manilla, is smelly and unattractive and a danger to the health of the poor who are condemned to live among it, but the rubbish of an emerging industrial society undoubtedly looks worse: rusty drums and discarded tyres and pools of oil and plastic containers, and such a veritable ocean of beer-cans that there is a move afoot to revert to returnable bottles.

We were lucky to be able to land at the airport, for the 'Harmattan' had just started. This is a seasonal wind from the north carrying dust from the desert, though, coupled with exhaust-fumes and the smoke from cooking-fires and industrial chimneys, it resembled nothing so much as an old-fashioned London pea-souper.

As we were flying out early next morning, weather permitting, to Enugu in the east, we were spared the five-hour drive to the city. Instead, we were accommodated at the Airport Hotel, adjacent to the airport and a mere hour's journey.

It is a shabby, rambling place. The long walk to our room took us through bleary neon-lit foyers, and along tin-roofed open walkways redolent of prison, a smell Jean Genet describes as composed of 'Piss, paint and paraldehyde'. The ceiling was down in the corridor, the air-conditioning was noisy but ineffectual, and the fumes from bald carpets and soft furnishings quietly rotting with the humidity was strong and offensive. The beds were clean and comfortable, there was brown running water in the well-appointed bathroom, and none of these complaints would have been of the slightest importance to us if the charge for the room had not been thirty pounds a night.

Sue was pondering whether the bath-water would be cleansing or the opposite when we were plunged into darkness. I popped my head round the door into the corridor, and there was not a chink of light to be seen. Fumbling my way to the window I saw that the city under the Harmattan was as dark as on the day of creation.

'It'll come on again in a minute,' I blethered half to myself, searching in vain for a candle with my cricket lighter, but the minutes ticked by, and sitting side by side on the bed our conversation languished in the absolute blackness, till only the sound of our stomachs rumbling broke the fog-blanketed silence.

'Do you think we could feel our way to the dining-room?' Sue whispered, as people do in the dark.

'They surely won't be serving.'

'It's better than sitting here like moles in a hole. We might find a sandwich.'

So, flicking the lighter on and off, we ventured forth clinging together, and inched our way along the dank passage.

We had heard that during the dry season thousands of spiders weave their webs in the overhead power-cables. When the rains come the whole city fuses, and they have to send out teams of workers armed with feather dusters.

As we reached the corner, through the haze we saw a glow surrounded by a faint orange halo. Then two. Then a blaze. The rest of the hotel was in full swing. The Harmattan had deceived us into thinking that the whole of Lagos was suffering from a power failure, when a faulty switch had blown a fuse in our wing.

*

Our companion on the flight the next morning was an Irish leprechaun with a Doctorate in Physical Efficiency. He was posing as an athlete's coach, though he looked as if he would blow over in a high wind, and he informed us that he had represented his country at the Olympics in Mexico in 1968, and that he held the world record for non-stop exercise – one hundred hours of assorted jerks.

On landing, Sue and I were preparing our royal wave for the photographers whom we had spied surging onto the landing-strip as the steps were wheeled into position, only to be roughly bundled out of the way while they flashed and clicked and smothered our little doctor in handshakes and fervent embraces. Quite right too.

Just as we were beginning to feel abandoned, our British Council Rep., Linda, pushed through the crowd, engulfing us in her enthusiasm, and drove us with Nigerian panache (which reduces all visitors to cringing blobs), to her lovely house among flowering jacarandas and frangipani in the residential suburbs of Enugu, the capital of that part of Nigeria which it is no longer tactful to call Biafra.

Over a 'hot' drink in tall glasses clinking with ice (for 'cold' here means soft drinks, while 'hot' means anything with spirits in it), we studied our plans for the next two weeks. Two performances every day except Sunday, frequently travelling long distances between each, which is perfectly feasible if one is giving a lecture, but in this climate our programme was too ambitious for such a schedule. We agreed to try it for the first week, with the option of cancelling or amalgamating performances thereafter, or, as a last resort, cutting and re-adapting the show. We were reluctant to do this, as 'the big guns' which were the most exhausting passages were also the most popular.

In our talks in London, the British Council had gleaned that we were keen to stay with African families wherever possible. Linda told us that for the following week we were to be guests of Mrs Okongwu, the mother of an Ibo friend, in a mud compound in a sprawling village in the forest, called Nnewe. Linda would be coming with us, and lest we should find the unfamiliar food unpalatable, Shadrach, her cook, would be accompanying us.

That night I dreamt of eating Missionary Pie, and it tasted of moth-balls.

*

The roads in this part of Nigeria are badly maintained. The tarmac, after years of heavy traffic and the annual rains, has dwindled to an irregular strip down the middle, wide enough for one vehicle only, which ends in a jagged cliff, beyond which lie unreliable verges of pitted red earth or shifting sand. Since what remains of the metalled surface affords the most comfortable passage, drivers approaching from opposite directions are reluctant to relinquish the centre till the last moment, which can be alarming for the chicken-hearted. It is said that cowards die a hundred deaths and brave men only once. After my experience of driving in Nigeria, I know to which category I belong. I have white hairs to prove it.

One hour from Enugu, and about the same distance from our first school, Rufus, the Ibo driver of our heavily loaded station-wagon, took aim in the approved manner at the mascot above the radiator of a fast-approaching saloon car. Unfortunately, he did not succeed in persuading the oncoming driver that our determination matched his, so that we had to capitulate rather later than was circumspect. We took off over the cliff-edge to land with a sickening crunch in a treacherous crater, shearing off a wheel.

Even on Safari the show must go on. We couldn't disappoint all those children. Leaving Rufus to see to the car, we unloaded all our luggage and stood with it in piles around us by the passing traffic.

Though I had seen countless open trucks, or 'Mammy Wagons' as they are called, bulging with Mammies taking livestock and assorted produce to the market, and bearing painted mottoes on

the side, 'GOD IS GOD', 'EVER ONWARDS – YES, AND BACKWARDS', 'QUEEN MUMMY JU-JU', I had no idea that one could hail them like a taxi, and climb aboard if there was room. 'GOD'S GRACE' squealed and huffed to a halt. Through the latticed super-structure the wagon looked full, and its occupants, without exception, surprised, but Linda and Shadrach negotiated with the driver, and within minutes the tailboard was down, people were heaving at our cases, we were yanked aloft and we were on our way, wedged in the middle of a jolting, juddering, noisy, scruffy truck-load of laughing humanity. We arrived at the school half an hour late, which in Nigeria is early.

After our second performance, the car was once more road-worthy. In a rust-red dusk, distant contours still soft with the mist of the departing Harmattan, trickling and itchy with prickly-heat, we set out for our first night 'in the bush', and only Linda knew the way through the intersecting maze of jungle paths. The great corrugated-iron gates of the mud compound opened at our approach. Chinwe, a buxom, rollicking girl of about twenty, stood caught in our headlights, her hair plaited and coiled into a coronet-like cage, her ears resplendent with tinkling silver rings. As we bumped over the last gulley, a deep moat carved by the rains, there was a harsh cry. In the sweeping lights we caught a fleeting glimpse of a chicken held across a stone having its head sliced off. Was it Ju-Ju or cuisine? Hibiscus flashed scarlet over a bowered terrace. Chinwe's mother and our hostess, Mrs Okon-gwu, came to meet us wearing a richly patterned wrapper and an extravagant bandanna.

'Good evening. You are welcome.' Even strangers we passed in the forest waved and shouted, 'You are welcome!'

We sat outside in the chirruping dark, waves of heat still rising from the baked earth, and Sue really tried not to flinch at the buzz of assorted bugs that were attracted by the single oil-lamp casting a faint glow up into Mrs Okongwu's face. We quenched our thirst with fresh palm-wine, which I had learned to tolerate, though when I first tried it in Sierra Leone it tasted like suds drained from sweaty vests. When it is fresh it is hardly intoxicating at all, but when it has been left to stand for only a matter of hours the effect is similar to being hit on the head with a rubber mallet.

Mrs Okongwu put her hands together and leant towards us solicitously.

'Now, my friends. I want to ask you whether you would prefer hot or cold water for your bath. You will want to wash before eating, I am sure.'

We had seen shadows passing to and fro with pots and basins spilling over on their heads, and Chinwe was crouched on her stool by the cooking fire, from which already emanated the de-liciously familiar smell of frying onions. Not wishing to delay the meal, and anxious to avoid any fuss on our behalf, we insisted on 'cold'. It was only later we discovered that 'hot' is the water that has been standing all day in the sun, and is the easiest to provide. 'Cold' is from jars buried deep in the ground, with thick lids, which are also used as ''fridges''.

With the dignity of a duchess, Mrs Okongwu said, 'I am now going to crack a joke.' We were all ears, but contrary to our expectations she launched into an ineffably sweet and unselfconscious rendering of 'Where, oh where has my Highland Laddie gone', which she had learnt as a child at Mission School. We asked if she could crack any jokes in Igbo, and she obliged us with a song which she translated as she went along, about an orphan boy and a magic custard-apple. At the risk of sounding sarcastic or insincere, I will say that at that moment I had the kind of revelation that we sometimes have in dreams. In the morning it isn't so convincing, but you think you have found the answer to the mystery of life. 'Cracking jokes' and custard-apples on Mrs Okongwu's terrace seemed quite close to it.

Chinwe came, smiling as always, wrinkling her nose and flashing her flawless teeth, to tell us our bath was ready. In the dark, I nearly knocked myself cold on the lintel of the little doorway. Chinwe gasped and said, 'Oh, sorry!' In Nigeria, this is a conditioned reflex to any misadventure. It has the unintended effect of making one feel clumsy. Ladling the cold water over ourselves with half a gourd in the spotless little cubicle by the gentle light of a hurricane lamp hanging from the rough wooden door was like morphine for pain.

We unpacked the mosquito-nets from the station wagon, and fixed them up while dinner was being prepared. The flavour of the stew, which they call 'soup', was exceptionally good, though I would not have believed that chicken could be cooked to have the consistency of a fast squash-ball. They like their meat 'al dente'. It accounts for their dazzling smiles.

We retired early, unaware of the demented rooster caged outside our 'window'. He started announcing the dawn at 11.35 p.m. precisely, and hardly paused for breath throughout the night, challenging a response from all the other demented roosters in the surrounding compounds, and setting off little chortles and gurgles among the hens. Above the chirruping of the cicadas and the raucous braying of toads, all night long a wood-dove bleeped away like the 'engaged' signal, subliminally bringing the frustration of the city into the heart of the jungle.

In the morning we could scarcely believe our eyes. Clean, rock-hard earth, almost polished with sweeping and the passage of bare feet. Baby goats the size of toy poodles nibbling in a heap of greenery. Mud outhouses, with soft organic lines, banana trees and plantains and pineapples and higgledy-piggledy palms. Thatched walls painted in dots and dags and geometrical designs. Chinwe pounding yams with a huge pestle and mortar, even in the cool of the morning, her strong shoulders glistening with sweat. The sound of children chanting from a 'kindergarten' outside the walls.

After breakfast of 'pap', which looks like mayonnaise and tastes ghastly, and 'bean-cakes', a delicious kind of savoury doughnut, washed down with palm-wine even at that early hour since I had expressed a liking for it, we took off with Rufus in the station wagon for our first school of the day.

Sue looked pristine in her borrowed nightie, her hair floating again after our therapeutic bucket-bath. My beard felt rather too thick and shaggy for *Macbeth*, though quite fitting for Shylock.

We were lurching along, happily disintegrating, as the great leveller, sweat, was starting to restore us to our normal, lank state, when there was a deafening explosion a few feet from the laterite road. Rufus, not the most phlegmatic of Ibos at the best of times, tried to drive up a cottonwood tree. Fortunately he was unsuccessful, as he was in most of his ventures, and we remained grounded. When the dust cleared, we saw a very un-warlike group of middle-aged ladies dancing to the music of a strange orchestra. A wizened patriarch was blowing into an ancient elephant-tusk, worn and aged to the colour of polished amber. A naked child, his belly embellished with an umbilical hernia like a walnut-whirl, was helping the old man to support the weight, while wiping his feet in the dust to the beat of the drums. A group of four men sat around a wooden xylophone, their enthusiasm bordering on frenzy. They appeared not so much to be playing it, as to be trying to demolish it. The deep-bass honking from the tusk reverberated in one's innards, producing a curious 'angst', which was no doubt the intention, as Rufus explained that the occasion was a

'Memorial Service' for the dead. Another 'firework' went off like a maroon. Sue clapped her hand over her good ear, but managed to smile. One woman held a picture of the departed high above her head, weaving and wailing and swinging her considerable backside about, to the danger of the children, whose concentration on keeping clear of rolling rumps had diminished with our arrival. The photograph depicted an elderly black Boadicea in a towering bandanna seated by a petrol pump. One very old lady launched into a display of uninhibited sexuality which was like a cry of anguish for the lost, lascivious days of her youth. They all seemed a little drunk, and far from sad. They were delighted when we stuck Kobos (Nigerian paper money) to their sweat-beaded foreheads – the traditional way of saying 'thank you' – and they danced on with renewed enthusiasm, waving and shouting, 'You are welcome!' as we had to leave for our morning 'matinée'. Two more bombs sent us on our way.

We found the school, and paid our de rigueur visit to the principal's office. We had had to learn diplomatically to curtail the pleasantries in the morning, as we often had a long drive in the heat of the day and lunch before our afternoon show.

It was a girls' school, and the audience was already assembled. As we entered from the back of the hall, the tightly packed rows of heads looked like an ornamental fringe, layers of decorative pom-poms, parted and plaited and teased into elaborate patterns. In a country where the British are expected to wear short back and sides, a shirt and a tie, I must have appeared a disreputable figure, with long hair, a red woolly beard, and a wide-brimmed, battered hat. Sue, at least, was a northern blonde goddess, apart from a few strands of very mortal hair clinging to her damp forehead, though it would no doubt have confused them if they had realised that she was dressed for bed. They clutched their texts and clung together, expecting the worst. One girl lost the fight to contain her mirth, and politely buried her laughter in her neighbour's pneumatic bosom.

The principal scampered ahead, eager to show us the curtain the girls had rigged up, made of patched bed-sheets and strung across the stage at a level that would have effectively concealed us from the tits down. Being reluctant to hurt their feelings, we agreed to be introduced with the two Amazons allotted to the task heaving at the rickety pulleys either side of the platform, a coup de théâtre which would at least surprise them with our bodies, though our heads would be clearly visible from the start unless we were to give at the knees. It would be disadvantageous, but not insuperable, to have to throw our lines across the rope like a shuttlecock in a badminton match – but suddenly it occurred to us. We liked to play as close as possible to our audience, and half of the best bits were set on the forestage, i.e. in front of the curtain line. We should either have to duck, which could detract from the dignity of a tragic hero, or be garotted. With apologies we suggested that it might be safer to dismantle the curtain.

'All we need is three chairs,' Sue explained, and we could see the doubt creeping across the principal's open face, that two hot Europeans, with no spinning plates or funny hats or indeed any evidence whatever of suitable paraphernalia, could possibly *entertain* all those children, some of whom had travelled miles to experience revelation in the field of drama. 'And somewhere to change.' A ray of hope illuminated the head mistress's features, though she was apologetic about the large cupboard filled with sacks of maize which was the only privacy she could provide.

'That's perfect,' we assured her. We liked a little seclusion, not only to preserve our precarious dignity, but also to surprise the children when we emerged, we hoped, transformed, in our improvised costumes.

The girls crowded round us at the end, as they frequently did, shyly asking for our addresses. Albinos are common in this part of Africa. One such, her white face a startling contrast to her dyed black hair, squinted at us through her blonde lashes and said, 'I want to be an actress. Can you tell me the secret?'

*

I lay on the nun's bed and mused about missionaries. There was a picture of Dürer's 'Hands in Prayer' on the table, along with slim religious booklets and an ivory rosary. The only concession to vanity in the bare room was a tiny mirror on the wall with a sentimentally illuminated text above it, 'I Am the Way'. We had lunched with three Sisters who were nurses in a fever hospital: Chantal, an ebullient French Canadian, who had spent ten years in Africa without losing an ounce of her original pioneering enthusiasm, Rosemary, a young, aristocratic-looking mouse, and Theresa, a thin-lipped Irish nun who blushed when she offered me her bedroom to rest in before setting off for our second performance. Though unable to sleep, we appreciated the chance to relax, and, above all, to avoid polite conversation. Though we were keenly curious, there were times when we longed for solitude to re-charge our batteries.

I deplore religious proselytising. The missionaries' legacy has often in the past been at best a superimposition of alien taboos on already superstitious societies, causing confusion and guilt. But, from my experience, the practice today has moved a long way from the theory of yesterday. I have respect and admiration for the missionaries we met, mostly teachers, whose beliefs I do not share, but who are undogmatic in their Catholicism or their Methodism or whatever, and who cheerfully devote their lives to the service of others less fortunate than their own countrymen. Their reward shows in their eyes. They are undoubtedly a blessedly happy lot, and their goodness is beyond dispute.

'Give me nuns any day,' Sue said, as we limply re-packed our costumes which had failed to dry out during our siesta. With two performances a day, we frequently had to go on stage feeling clammy and smelling dank. 'They're so mercifully self-contained.'

We had found that many of the Europeans we had met had lost the art of conversation. Deprived of new faces, they tended to bend one's ear remorselessly for as long as one could take it without shouting for help. It was as if the climate had given them the verbal runs.

'I think Sister Theresa fancies me,' I said. 'She never stops blushing, and she gave me an extra helping of semolina.'

'You flatter yourself. It's me she fancies.'

'That's in bad taste.'

'Why? Just because she's a nun? You're such a puritan at heart.'

'This conversation is taking a surrealistic turn. I suggest we drop it, and talk about something safe, like politics or religion.'

At the next school we played in a second-storey dining hall with walls reaching only half-way to the roof. They had improvised a precarious stage from dozens of narrow, uneven benches.

As we wobbled and lurched through the Banquet Scene in *Macbeth*, we were arrested by the sight of sixty pairs of eyes gazing astounded at us from the branches of two enormous jacaranda trees just beyond the eaves. We wobbled on bravely. Suddenly there was a loud crack and a hideous rending noise, and the air was black with thrashing limbs as all the branches seemed to break at once. Turning with ill-considered haste to see if assistance was needed, Sue caught her heel in a space between the benches, and our improvised stage collapsed about our knees like a pack of dominoes, wrenching my ankle and bruising Sue's elbow. Everyone shouted 'Oh, sorry!' at once, and rushed to our assistance. Outside, the casualties turned out to be nil, so we finished the show on the flat, and were greeted at the end with a storm of cheers.

✻

The house behind ours in Mrs Okongwu's compound was beautifully maintained and conspicuously artistic. The flowing lines of its burnished mud walls were newly painted in an emerald-green interlocking triangle motif, with intricate patterns in deep purple superimposed. The doorway was scarlet, and from it on our return that evening emerged a tall woman with a loping stride, bearing a cornucopia of fruit on her head, a wooden bowl containing bananas, mangoes, oranges, and a large pineapple. She presented us with the fruit, holding her hands up in a balletic gesture of astonishment, dipping her knees and swaying in a curious dance. 'No!' she kept saying, and, though she was smiling, she seemed to get cross. 'No! No! NO!'

'No?' I asked, offering hesitantly to return the fruit, eat it, or indeed do whatever would placate her rising wrath.

Mrs Okongwu arrived just as the situation was becoming sticky, carrying a tray of 'Star' and groundnuts.

'Mrs Odela speaks no English,' she explained. 'She is saying "Noh!" Noh! means "You are welcome" in Igbo.'

'Ah!' we said. 'Thank you. Thank you very much.' And we bowed in return, and the lady let out a long 'Eyhh!' of joy as she saw the pleasure that her gift had brought us.

Thereafter we said 'Noh!' indiscriminately to everyone, and though, strictly speaking, we were the guests and the Ibos were our hosts, it went down very well.

Chinwe was such an excellent cook that Shadrach's services were not needed over the cooking fire, and I can vouch that our jungle fare had no ill-effects on our digestive systems. In Sue's case, this might have been partly due to an incident that happened that night after we had retired. She had occasion to pay a nocturnal

visit to the 'thunder box'. It turned out to be an effective deter-
rent to developing the runs. It was, in fact, a deep pit, surmounted by a scrubbed wooden box-seat, in a scrupulously
clean mud cubicle, but in the small hours of the morning it
became a meeting place for creatures of whom Sue was particularly unfond, spiders of a size she had never previously encountered. She claims she didn't have a movement for a week.

As the treble bleating of the goats and the crowing of the
roosters, and the laughter of the girls as they fetched water and
pounded yams and prepared the fire for breakfast, was not con-
ducive of indolence, we were up in time to accompany Mrs
Okongwu on her first-light tour of the village.

Girls sweeping, goats nibbling, babies feeding, women pounding. Charred hollows, where they extract the oil from the
porcupine-prickly fruit of the palm. A semi-spherical ju-ju
ceremonial mound, containing magic not to be spoken of. Plaited
fences and walls thatched with palm-fronds to keep out the rains.
Saucer-eyed waifs taking startled refuge behind their mother's
skirts. 'Ngwu', the Holy Tree that bestows fertility on the devout,
if prayed to. The life-sized effigies of a man and a woman propped
up on the roof of an overgrown ruin, he with a solar topee tipped
rakishly over his livid forehead, for the faces of both were painted
a ghastly white...another memorial to the dead. Though their
bleached appearance has no racial significance, here, in the heart
of Black Africa, white is the colour of sickness and death. Everyone we met, man, woman and child, shouted, 'Noh! You are
welcome! Noh, noh! You are welcome!'

Finally Mrs Okongwu guided us in the direction of a pros-
perous-looking, well-cared-for compound. Astride the high wall
was a portly gentleman in baggy shorts, amid a quivering
thicket of palm-fronds, which he was weaving into thatch with
some dexterity.

'Ah!' he beamed. 'You are welcome,' and slid instantly from
sight into his compound.

'This is our chief, Mr Christian Obi,' Mrs Okongwu introduced us. In the time it had taken for the gates to be opened,
Mr Obi had changed from his working-clothes into the flowing
robes of his people.

'We must break Kola,' he said, escorting us across the gently undulating yard to the terrace of his house, where we sat under an aching cascade of crimson bougainvillea, while the chalk and the Kola, the traditional symbols of welcome among the Chiefs of the Ibos, were produced.

We explained that, being so recently arrived from England, we were ignorant of their customs.

'Then let me show you, my friends,' he said. He lifted one of two carved wooden dishes. In the middle was a hollow the size of a saucer filled with a worn cake of white chalk. With his fore-finger he smeared a stripe of it on the inside of each of our wrists. Though it didn't show up on our pallid complexions, he was undismayed.

'The chalk is a visible sign that you are one of us, and while you are among the Ibos you will come to no harm. And now you should accept the Kola, thus and thus...' He instructed us to lay our hands over the other dish, which contained a little nut, segmented like an orange but no bigger than a walnut. This we did, while he explained that no woman could 'break' the nut into its segments. The senior man present must do it, so with a charming homily on the brotherhood of man, which was wise and thoughtful and far from naïve, Mr Obi 'broke' the nut and passed the ceremonial dish around. The Kola nut is a bitter-tasting mild stimulant, like coffee, which is dipped, before eating, into molten metal, which they call pepper sauce. There were tears in our eyes when we left, though even Mr Obi must have deduced that they were not the result of undiluted emotion, for Sue was still clutching her throat, and my tongue was lapping at the morning air like a puppy towards its master.

*

Our morning performance in Owerri was delayed by an hour and a half, which may well have saved our lives. The school had erected an admirable stage in the middle of a field. It would have been an exciting challenge to play 'in the round', but due to transport problems and unreliable roads the outlying schools had not arrived. As the sun crept inexorably higher, and the temperature rose towards boiling-point, we realised that, had we started at the scheduled time, we would by then have been frying like sacrificial victims. Without so much as a square-inch of shadow, after two hours of unremitting passion we should surely have collapsed. The children too, though used to the sun, would have been desperately uncomfortable.

There was time and the opportunity to change the venue to the front of the principal's house, where we later played on his pillared porch, while the pupils crammed into the dappled shade of the garden. It was one of the most felicitous performances we gave, marred only by two incidents.

The occasion of our appearance at these remote places being unprecedented, the conscientious staff were anxious to keep order for our sakes in the established manner. At the first sign of laughter or chat, a teacher would leap to his feet swinging a clangorous school-bell. This reduced the listeners to well-behaved, suffering students, and us to privileged pedants. Comedy scenes were a write-off, and rapport was at its lowest. We felt that it nullified our whole endeavour.

After it first happened, we used to ask for the bell before each performance. We would hold it aloft, and, at the sight of it, the audience subsided into submissive silence, and one could see them prepare for another joyless bout of long-suffering obedience. We would then ask a pupil to remove it from the hall, and we assured them that in our performance it would never be rung. It may have been sneaky, but it got them on our side, and we never regretted it. But in the bustle of re-arranging the stage at the last moment in Owerri, we had omitted to go through this little charade, and the bell clanged all the way through *Macbeth* like a fire-engine looking for a fire. Between plays, we begged the headmaster to discard it, and assured him that we could cope with what they called rowdiness, and what we called response.

There was one practice, however, which we had no power to discourage: that of whipping the children. It was not done with sadistic relish, but it was nevertheless offensive to our sensibilities. When the hall was full, or the garden in this instance, a teacher or a prefect would stand by the entrance with a long stick, or a whip of rhinoceros hide, and swipe at the legs of importunate youngsters still pressing to enter. Their squeals disturbed us, and on more than one occasion I had to restrain Sue from storming through the throng to snatch these weapons from those wielding them and break them across her shapely knee.

We lunched with our first mixed marriage, and there were lots to come. He from Onitsha, she from Bolton, and there was more tenderness in evidence than one would expect in an ordinary British household: after ten years, a triumph on both sides of tolerance and understanding. The children were neither beautiful nor plain, but perhaps they will help to build a bridge to the future, with luck. I played 'Away in a Manger' on their harmonium, which I am wont to do when faced with a musical instrument – like territory demarcation among dogs.

*

We were hoist by our own petard. After the bell incident in the morning, feeling a little smug and well-pleased with ourselves, we were faced with the most unruly pack of young hooligans that it was our misfortune to encounter throughout our trip. Shout and bellow as we might, we could not make ourselves heard over the din without inviting laryngitis. The hall was too big for a start. Like many of the buildings we played in, it was badly bullet-scarred and minus windows, so that teachers guarding the entrances with whips were powerless to prevent hordes of children climbing through the window-spaces. Schools, being the most common solidly built edifices throughout the country, were frequently used as fortresses during the war.

All it needs in an audience of this size (we estimated about fifteen hundred), is one noisy element and the whole house is disrupted. They are probably noisy because they don't understand, but the ones who want to hear get aggressive towards the others, and bedlam ensues. We stopped and delivered a little speech, which they listened to, thank God.

'We are going to stop now, because we can't be heard and we are straining our voices. We have many more schools to play to, and if our voices go, those schools will also be deprived of hearing these plays, which we're sure most of you here today also want to hear. If you find it hard to understand, or boring, please leave now, as we cannot do the plays for you if we cannot be heard. You must understand, it is not like going to the cinema. We want you to enjoy yourselves, laugh where you want, and even talk a little, within reason, but we must have your help. For those of you who want to stay and listen, we shall start again in ten minutes.'

I would like to report that when we began again those who remained, the vast majority, were as quiet as mice. They were not, but we managed to plod through to the end, though it was a poor performance.

❋

Mrs Okongwu and Chinwe and the dancing-lady from the painted house and Mr Obi, supporting himself on an ornately carved black walking-stick, followed us out of the compound gates and stood waving after our departing car, the bright colours of their robes and wrappers like stained-glass windows in the cathedral-shade of the forest.

'Noh! You are welcome! Noh! Noh!'

We lurched along the track, clutching the presents they had brought, fruit, and dried fish, and new palm wine.

'And may God bless you and keep you!' Mrs Okongwu held her hands together, Chinwe wrinkled her nose, and the dancing lady went into a rousing finale, arms raised above her head, backside swinging riotously, and that was the last we saw of them as a cloud of dust rose behind our churning wheels.

❋

From truckle-beds in a mud compound to Dunlopillo divans and a private bath. From Igbo songs round a cooking-fire to amplified 'pop' in an 'English' garden. From bean-cakes and 'soup' and pepper sauce and mealies to a banquet like the shah's at Persepolis. In such contrasts lay the fascination of our tour.

During our week in the jungle we had started taking salt-tablets to strengthen our resilience, and they seemed to help – though by the evening we were usually dumb with fatigue. Cold liquid was our top priority; first, to immerse ourselves in, or throw over our tickling flesh; next, to imbibe in large quantities. What we looked forward to most at the end of a working day was not a party. We were spending the night with the headmistress of a girl's school, however, and she had invited the elite of Owerri to meet us.

Lots of cold water proved once again to be therapeutic, and our smiles quickly relaxed in genuine pleasure as we were introduced to the assembled company. Doctors and teachers and diplomats and businessmen, shy laconic wives and outspoken career-women, a composer, an engineer and a diminutive steward who rejoiced in the name of Paraffin Sandwich.

Originality is esteemed above tradition when naming a child. English names are often adopted in addition to African ones, since English, the lingua franca, is the only means of communication between the many tribes, each with its own language. In two months, we came across Hitler and Samson, Lovemore and Filament, Christian and Cosmos, Hyacinth and Flobert and Menthol, an elfin little albino with ribbons in her ginger hair called Astonishment, and identical twins called Plastic and Plaster.

Paraffin toddled among the guests filling glasses with ice-cold punch from a jug half as big as himself. A gigantic flame-tree in full flower was lit from below by twenty hurricane lamps set around its mighty trunk in a ghostly circle. Easy-chairs were placed beside them, and we helped ourselves to the prodigal buffet and sat in this most dramatic of settings, the scarlet blossom piling up above us into the night-sky like an infernal cumulus. It was perhaps no wonder that the conversation turned towards tragedy. They spoke of those who had died in the Biafran war, of the mass graves of their countrymen who had been killed or starved to death, and of the thousands upon thousands who had been left unburied in the blazing sun.

'Why?' Sue asked. 'Why weren't they buried?'

'No time,' said a kindly-looking man whose word we were inclined to believe, for he wore a dog-collar. 'The ants got them first.'

It was a chilling moment, and one we were to recall vividly in only a matter of weeks.

*

'They've laid on a party,' Sue said. 'There's a wild animal under the sink, and I'm sharing a bed with Linda.' There were tears in her eyes as she sat on the edge of mine, her shoulders hunched in despair. A week of travelling and playing and travelling and playing, and the salt-tablets had ceased to be a panacea for our exhaustion. We were lodging with a family in Abba, a sizeable town. The family was charming and numerous, though I never did discover how many there were as we arrived after dark and left at dawn. Inside the apartment, the total darkness was relieved by the feeblest glimmer from several electric wall-fittings, and I could only pick out our hosts and their children by the whites of their eyes.

'I'm sure they won't throw a fit if you sleep with me. Much as I love Linda,' I added, 'I can't offer to share with her.'

'Of course not. Oh, I'll be all right. It might offend them if we sleep together. It's not that – I can't face party chatter now. I just want to sleep for a week, have a wash, and there's a horrible great beast guarding the bath...'

The horrible great beast turned out to be a discarded pair of trousers, in the gloom, crouched ready to spring. There was no water in the pipes, but buckets and ladles were provided, which by this time we almost preferred. Bathed, and in fresh linen, we felt prepared for civilities, if not exactly prime for repartee.

'Happy Birthday, dear Thomas – Happy Birthday too-oo you!' We raised our glasses to the spherical gentleman at the head of the table on this, the occasion of his fiftieth birthday, and their gusts of rumbustious, musical laughter did more to perk us up than the excellent French champagne. The women, dressed in gowns of brilliant colours, some with bandannas over a foot high, others with hair plaited and coiled into a variety of styles, all sat demurely at one end of the table, while the men congregated at the other round Tom, the principal guest and a chief into the bargain. As the party got under way, we soon forgot that the chairs we were sitting on were rusty and squealed horribly when moved on the clinker underfoot, that the table-top was chipped Formica, and that we were the only customers in what seemed to be a large car-park.

The evening continued at 'The Club', a luxurious establishment, in the past for whites only, where we danced 'The High Life' beside a floodlit pool where a child had drowned the week before. And we reflected, without patronising, how Africans have a talent for extrovert joy that we seem to have lost, a spontaneous, infectious appetite for laughter which is not only good for the lungs, but good for the soul.

*

The smallest child looked no more than nine years old, but she juddered her buttocks with precocious sexuality. The girls came through the compound gate in sinuous single file, looking neither to left nor right, wafting a handkerchief, which must have been a leaf in the old days, in one hand, and weaving towards 'the band', who squatted over their drums in the middle of the courtyard. The bells round the girls' waists jingled with each step they took, and each arched her glistening back towards the ring of spectators.

This compound was a world away from our jungle home with Mrs Okongwu, Mr Obi, and the demented rooster. We were staying with a 'Paramount Chief', a chief among chiefs who, behind trimmed hedges dotted with crimson flowers, had built three handsome villas for himself and his sons. We had broken Kola in his upstairs lounge, sitting on fat velour easy-chairs, gazing out over the primaeval rain-forest. Though there was a shortage of water, there were buckets of sparkling hot and cold in our bathroom, soft towels on the rail, and a king-sized bar of Imperial Leather on the bathing-stool. The servants had snatched our soiled linen, and were bashing it merrily with wooden blocks below our window, beside a brimming basin and a large packet of Daz.

We had lunched off mealey-mealey and 'soup', with chicken and sweet potatoes and chilli sauce, the chief had opened a magnum of Spanish wine in our honour, and, as the relentless heat loosened its death-grip on the afternoon, the village maidens made their entrance to beguile us with their regimented passion.

For an hour they stamped to the rhythm of the pounding drums and clicking sticks, bowing and dipping and singing in piping harmony, each dance with a different beat, with different steps, with a different meaning, yet all with an emphasis it was impossible to ignore on that part of the anatomy which in England is reserved for schoolboy jokes and sitting on. It frequently looked as if it was being worked by wires, each shapely buttock twitching up into the air by turns, and quivering with a life of its own that was altogether surprising.

As the shadow of the giant palms crept across the courtyard, the little virgins finally left us; and the serious business of the afternoon behind them, they granted us the pleasure of their radiant smiles.

We set off with Pious, the chief's son, to visit a Ju-Ju shrine, a privilege rarely afforded to Europeans. We intercepted an urchin on the way, asking him to alert the high priest. Though we bumped and whined for some miles over the dusty paths by car, the priest, in the mysterious manner so often encountered in Africa, was already there when we arrived, his luminously intense face corrugated with tribal scars.

He led us through the gate along a winding path to the shrine, no bigger than a garden hut. A thatched roof sheltered carved figures painted in lurid colours, with baleful eyes and protruding organs, devils all, that could only inspire fear or disgust. The sacrificial drum was spattered with black dried blood, and stuck with feathers, which lifted in the eddying waves of heat, making it appear to move like a corpse infected with maggots. He explained, without the African equivalent of a blush, that unfortunately only chickens and goats could be slaughtered, which were pretty feeble medicine, since human sacrifice was now illegal.

In the evening, after the generator stopped, we sat with the chief and his sons on the upstairs terrace in a darkness that was almost tangible. Conversation with no need to show attention or interest takes on the intimacy of lovers' nocturnal confessions. For once, we didn't discuss politics or the war or racial tension. Instead we talked of multiple marriage and bringing up children and of the purely Western scourge of loneliness in old age. To be old in Africa is to be cherished and revered, and loneliness at any age is a state which, physically at least, does not exist.

Our Ibo friends had stripped to simple wrappers worn round the waist. Sue was curled up next to me in her nightgown, and I wore nothing but a towel. We were deliciously drowsy, revelling in the touch of the night-air on our nakedness, when the chief asked us if we had noticed the curious musky odour that pervaded the compound.

'It's the bats,' he explained with a disapproving rumble in his throat. 'This year they've reached plague proportions.'

I could feel Sue stiffen.

'As big as rats, some of them. We'll have to start exterminating them, Pious.'

'After the rains, father.'

We had been grateful for the little movements of air which, till that moment, we had taken for jungle zephyrs blowing a welcome breath on our exposed flesh. The knowledge of the bats' 'radar' was no comfort, as we started to imagine fanged creatures with the wingspan of a seagull plunging in a sinister silence about our heads. Without betraying our cowardice, we shortly made our excuses, and by the flame of my lighter we found our way to the bedroom.

We bolted the door, and Sue let out a groan of relief.

'Thank God we're inside,' she said. 'If a bat touched me I think I'd die.'

We lit the candle, and our eyes became adjusted to the gloom. Hanging upside down on the cord that supported the mosquito net were six black bats squirming in a cluster above the bed and twitching their tattered wings. Sue's screams brought the men running. They dislodged them from their perch, but they refused to be coaxed out into the night. They swooped from one corner to the other, the shadow of their erratic flight lapping huge and menacing over the walls. They stuck to the ceiling and wriggled along the beams and crept into inaccessible corners. Finally there was nothing to do but retire, tuck the net well in, and pray for the dawn.

*

In the morning we played in a dining-hall reeking of stale fat. We changed in the kitchen, which regaled the staff. By the roundness of the eyes peering over the banks of cookers, we deduced that this kind of dressing-up in general, and the wearing of jock-straps and tights in particular, was unknown to them. They soon lost control of their good manners, and clung helplessly together, generous bosoms heaving in unison, as their cackles and whoops reverberated off the tiled walls.

In the afternoon, the venue was a Methodist chapel, where we estimated that 'The quality of mercy...' was not too sacrilegious to deliver from the pulpit, though when it came to question time we were intimidated by the atmosphere of sanctity into forgoing our customary fag and litre bottle of Star beer.

In between we visited a large market, miles from any road, limping the last part in the suffocating heat of noon under a day-glo pink umbrella, past villages of thatched rondahvels inhabited by only the very old and the very young. The rest had gone to participate in the weekly orgy of buying and selling and gossip and wrangling which distinguishes African markets from their pallid European counterparts. As we approached the meeting place through the trees, it seemed a palette of garish colour against the sombre monotony of the forest.

Down a steep declivity, a pool in the mud-red river was frothing with the antics of a multitude of boys and girls frolicking like porpoises. Sue sat me down on the bank, and fished for her Instamatic to capture the moment in Living Blur, but before she had time to frame the picture they had spied us, the swirling water was empty, and we were surrounded by a dripping army of naked children, pulling at our clothes and fighting among themselves to get a closer look at the strange pink creatures who had suddenly appeared in their midst. The young ones had clearly never seen white people before. Their fear quite eclipsed their curiosity. They screamed or burst into tears if we approached them, or tried to touch their fluffy heads, though the persistence of the older ones prevented outright flight. Sue picked up a phlegmatic ball of black butter that had attached itself to her knee, and cuddling-being-seen-to-be-done did something to dispel their terror.

In our progress through the market we were followed like the Pied Piper. The adults shouted 'Beke', and the children took up the cry. Though it means 'White Man' it is a friendly greeting, derived from 'Baker', the name of the first white missionary to visit these parts. We bought some dried fish, evenly bound, like scales, onto a kite-shaped tray, half a dozen small black earthenware bowls, and the kernels of spiky-melons, that had the changing iridescence of opals. (Peeled and cooked, they are white, and taste like butter-beans.) An old man – Sue gets cross when I suggest he must have been drunk – knelt and kissed her feet, which caused her embarrassment more than pleasure. We did not shake off the last of our followers till we reached the road again, where Rufus was waiting to take us, after our show, to our next 'home', a modern bungalow outside the traditional village of Item, where our hostess was a dimpled ever-smiling mother of ten whom we had already met at Chief Tom's fiftieth birthday-party in the car-park.

Chapter Four

The Village

The Chalk Dish and the Kola Dish were the most ancient and elaborate I'd seen, though the bare mud hut contained only a simple bench and a wooden armchair without upholstery, polished with constant use. When eating the Kola, I 'mimed' the pepper sauce. Daniel, a local teacher, was taking me round the village, starting in the chief's hut. The chief was an old man, wearing a red and black woollen cap, which is the badge of his position in this part of Nigeria, and he spoke no English. He presented us with a yam half the size of a Gladstone bag, all gnarled and warty, which he handled with pride. Daniel felt it, and turned it over thoughtfully, then handed it back to me for appraisal. Several little girls, their hair done in 'worms', with babies half their own size strapped to their backs, crowded into the hut, followed by a jostling rearguard of naked toddlers with swollen bellies and moonstruck eyes. Everybody said 'Eyhh!' at regular intervals, and the young ones huddled against the knees of the old chief, hanging onto him with fistfuls of his robes. He was evidently no remote figure of authority.

We took our leave, and Daniel asked me if I should like to accompany him to a meeting in the village, over which, as a man of education, he was presiding. He was in the position of a magistrate, or arbiter, and the women had come to him with a grievance. It appeared that some men had been doing women's work, and, the social structure being rigidly divided into formal roles, the women felt, like a closed-shop trade-union, that this

95

'scab labour' impinged on their position in the village. Although both men and women take part in agriculture, the planting and harvesting of cassava, for example, is exclusively women's work, and men are rigorously forbidden from cultivating it, while, conversely, the care of the palm-tree and the handling of its products, oil and wine, are forbidden to the women.

The villagers were already assembled when we arrived at the long-hut as dusk was falling. It was perched on the crown of a grassy knoll, and it consisted of posts about twelve feet high set in a rectangle about forty feet long by twenty feet wide, supporting a thatched roof weighted with stones. Though I would have preferred to have been an unobtrusive observer, Daniel firmly sat me down on his right side at the single table, and I was flattered to realise that, coming from overseas, they considered me not an interloper but an important visitor. The elders sat on two benches on either side of us, some with their hands folded above finely carved walking-sticks. Some younger men sat on a bench in front of us, while others lent against the posts, or stood around in groups silently reverential. Children, who are normally everywhere in evidence, were nowhere to be seen. They had either been banned from attending such weighty proceedings, or else, through experience, they had found them boring. The women glided in silently, and squatted in a tight group on the ground in the far corner.

Daniel read the petition by the light of a torch, though, while he delivered a short speech, a hurricane lamp was placed on the table, which lit our immediate vicinity, and by contrast obliterated the rest of the company. Speakers from the body of the meeting became disembodied voices. When the 'palaver' was heated, a steward with a wooden 'bell' – a hollowed-out tree-trunk, with a thigh-bone as a clapper – drowned the babble with this imperious instrument. (I thought of our school-bell, and was pleased to note its origin.) An ancient scribe, skinny as a whippet, dressed in sky-blue robes, took down the minutes as well as he could, though he kept falling asleep across the table, once singeing himself cruelly on the lamp. Some of the elders, leaning on their sticks, dozed throughout, swaying very gradually to the nodding point-of-balance then back again, like slow-motion metronomes.

After interminable speeches, of which I understood not a word, there was a specially rousing peal on the bell, and Daniel took me outside by the arm.

Thank God it's over, I thought, for though I was fascinated by the people, the incomprehensible dialogue was becoming tedious. Dashing my hopes, however, Daniel explained that he was suspending the meeting for ten minutes to allow private discussion before voting.

The evening, though starless, seemed brilliant, vibrating with the high-pitched trilling of thousands of cicadas, and the lamps from the night-market far below twinkled as clearly as Golden Rain bursting before our faces.

'Excuse me, John, if you please,' Daniel asked, and I presumed from his apologetic manner that he wished to relieve himself. Instead, he produced a small box from about his person by sleight of hand, and carefully opened it. He dug his forefinger into what it contained, and retrieved it, bearing on the end an amount of brown powder roughly equivalent to a large teaspoonful. He then, without warning, rammed this substance up his left nostril like gunpowder into a blunderbuss. After he had repeated the action for his right nostril, I, being in the heart of Darkest Africa, doubted whether the substance was as innocuous as snuff, which it turned out to be, but above all I was flabbergasted at the quantity of it that had disappeared inside his face.

There was a dazzling flash of sheet-lightning, which splashed the whole village for a second in a wash of wan, flat light, and in the darker darkness that ensued there was not a hint of thunder. After a decorous sneeze, Daniel led me back towards the unfinished business.

It was the women's turn. A gentle matriach delivered a long impassioned plea in a reticent, beautifully modulated contralto, and the whole meeting gave her its undivided attention. The vote was taken, after which Daniel made a speech, which he explained afterwards was simply an apology, followed by a prayer. I know this, because he used the only word I understood throughout the meeting, 'Amen'.

The meek, downcast women shuffled silently to their feet, but as they started making their way down the hill towards the village they burst into a triumphant Ibo song in four-part harmony, the intermittent, silent flashes of lightning illuminating their rhythmically swaying procession.

Putting my hand on his shoulder, Daniel led me like a blind man over the uneven ground towards his hut. On the way he told me that he had only recently re-married. He was a devout Christian and he was most anxious to assure me that he was monogamous, and genuinely sad that the only reason he had had to take another wife was because his first wife was barren.

In the shadows cast by a single oil-lamp his child-bride sat immobile like a captured gazelle. A naked infant was at her breast, with the all too frequent umbilical hernia crowning his fat tummy. We shared a glass of beer while we talked of education, and he lamented over the agonising dearth of books and facilities and materials in Ibo country. He felt that the Ibos were being deprived by the Federal Government as a punishment for starting the war...

In the flashing dark he led me to a candle-lit stall in the market, where he bought a battery for his torch. I could then relinquish his shoulder.

'We still pray to the rain-gods,' he confided on the way home. The air was heavy, like a wet, warm balloon, but still the lightning followed by silence seemed to promise no respite for the thirsty land.

'Do you think it will rain, John?'

'*I* don't know, Daniel!' I laughed to think that he sincerely appeared to value my opinion. 'But with no thunder, I shouldn't think just yet.'

A splash of water quite two inches in diameter landed in a puff of dust in the beam at our feet. The next landed on my head, as if a cup had been emptied from the branches of a tree above us. Within minutes we were floundering through a wall of water, and the noise of it hitting the leafy undergrowth and pouring into the foaming mud which had been dust a moment before drowned the night in a swirling cataract.

When you are drenched to the skin in the first five minutes, it is thoroughly enjoyable to squelch through the 'Mango' rains with the thought of 'home' at the end of it. These little rains herald the start of the rainy season, and are so called because the mangoes ripen at this time.

The deluge only lasted an hour, but it had done for the generator and the cooking fire, so we ate 'cold-table' by candle-light, washed down with milky fresh palm-wine.

The air after the storm was no longer sultry. There was distant thunder now, crashing over the forest where the stars glittering above us faded behind the receding curtain of cloud.

'Could you eat a man if you had to?' Sue asked. We were standing by the bedroom window, revelling in the elemental smell of the quenched earth.

'With H.P. sauce,' I quipped, quick as a flash. 'I can eat anything with H.P. sauce. And some soggy chips.'

'Because Chijoke and Ojuku have.'

'But they're children!'

They were the sons of the household, nineteen and twenty respectively, all sparkling teeth and twinkling eyes and dressed to the nines in flared trousers and six-inch platform-soled boots and waisted shirts and chunky jewellery, the admired mode among the young in Nigeria, though usually deplored by their elders.

While I had been attending the meeting, Sue had spent the time watching the leisurely flight of fireflies sparkling in the bushes in the company of these young '70s dandies, on the porch of our bungalow overlooking the village. In this idyllic situation, their tales of the war seemed unreal and far-fetched. They spoke with pride of killing Hausas before they were into their teens, and with no bitterness or shame of eating them when they were starving. They had survived.

'Have you heard the story of the Ibo, the Hausa and the Yoruba sitting under a coconut tree?' Ojuku had asked.

Sue waited.

'The Yoruba says, "I wish a coconut would fall. I am thirsty for its milk!" The Hausa says, "If it is Allah's will, it will fall." The Ibo climbs the tree, fetches an armful of coconuts, and sells them to the other two.'

And they could still laugh like schoolboys.

＊

The teacher scribbled on the wall in the absence of a blackboard, and the children sat on bricks, using rough-hewn planks as desks.

They struggled to their feet as we entered, chorusing 'Good-morning Sirs. Good-morning Miss.' Their faces so open and unguarded, registering only superlative emotions, amazement and terror, then crumpling into smiles of infectious joy. Sue was so busy simpering with unalloyed delight that she tripped over a pupil's school-box, which they carry on their heads like everything else, and the entire class in unison muttered 'Oh, sorry!'

In the seclusion of an overgrown ruin we changed back to back, not for reasons of modesty, but to keep a three hundred and sixty degree lookout for snakes. The performance was notable not only for the uninhibited response from these village children, who were rather younger than most of our audiences had been, but also, since we were playing in a shady glade in the open which formed a natural amphitheatre, for the unexpected appearance in Belmont of a scruffy little bitch on heat dragging her sated consort behind her yelping piteously. A few well-aimed stones from the bigger boys sent them both still joined together on their way.

*

The long drive back to Enugu was eventful. The heavens opened once more, and an over-loaded Mammy-wagon, which we had been unable to overtake, slid quite gently off the top of the tarmac cliff ahead of us and turned upside down. With towels over our heads to absorb the onslaught of the downpour, we heaved for all our worth at the visible arms and legs poking through the ruptured superstructure. The shrieks and moans of those trapped inside were heart-rending, and I feared there would be many casualties. In ten minutes, however, they were all out, shouting and laughing and railing at the driver who held up his hands in despair, while the deluge sizzled on his upturned truck. One little boy clutched his arm which had started to swell, and which we feared might be broken, but he refused our offer to take him to a hospital, and as no one claimed him, or was prepared to accompany him, we had to leave him be. We reported the accident at the next town.

We passed herds of graceful humped cows with fly-away horns, being driven north by their beautiful Fulani herders, the women with painted eyes, and clinking with silver ornaments. Due to the prevalence of tsetse-fly in the south, cattle cannot be bred there.

The rain stopped. On rounding a bend we almost thumped into the scraggy flanks of a hundred horses on their way to a market by the roadside. Horses are rare, also due to the tsetse-fly, and are favoured for ceremonial occasions and sacrifice above other animals. When a chief or a distinguished citizen dies, to club a horse to death in his honour is a sacrifice worthy of a great man, and 'Horse-Killer' is an epithet won and dearly prized by those who best perform this grisly rite. Despite our Ju-Ju priest's lament that human sacrifice is illegal, recently an important chief was buried with seven soldiers' heads to accompany him on his last journey.

We ran out of petrol. Since there was an acute shortage our plight would have been serious, had not Rufus flashed his British Council badge and talked airily of Ambassadors and International Relations and twenty thousand disappointed children. The springs collapsed. We had to reduce our speed radically, and thereafter we all had to disembark at the bigger craters and cross the uneven plank bridges on foot. The exhaust fell off. We limped into Enugu after nightfall, scattering chickens and goats and children of assorted sizes in an ear-splitting fusillade. Linda's tended lawns in the dazzle of our headlights were like the Elysian Fields.

*

'What's wrong with murdering Duncan in the Gentlemen's loo?' I asked tetchily. 'It's off right! The Gents is perfect.'

The layout of the courtyard where it was projected that we should give our 'Gala Performance' for adults that evening was ideal, except that there were only two ways of getting on and off the acting area – from the Gents at one side, and the Ladies at the other. We always very specifically 'placed' the events which took place off-stage, like the murder of Duncan, so that the audience could imagine the king's bloody corpse lying in some chamber just beyond the exit.

'*I* don't mind, so long as it's not actually in use during the performance,' Sue said. 'It could cause confusion, my bursting in on people on the point of relieving themselves, wringing my hands. Apart from your "Who's there? What ho?" '

'What *about* my "Who's there? What ho?" '

'Well, you do shout it quite loud, love, off right I mean. And if the place is in use they could miss their aim.'

'We'll cover up the signs and make an announcement, asking them to restrain themselves till the interval.'

There was a gallery running round three sides of the yard, and our little stage jutted out into the middle of the audience. When we arrived at night, the stage was flooded with two follow-spots, manned by British Council employees; they had provided us with three elegant chairs, the 'Ladies' and 'Gents' signs were cunningly concealed behind red velvet banners, and the crowded auditorium under the stars looked for all the world as if it had been designed as an Elizabethan theatre. The colourful gowns of both men and women, the dinner-jackets and evening-dresses of the less traditional, and the sparkle of jewellery on dusky throats, was a stirring sight after our rustic Odyssey.

'I'm nervous!' Sue confessed, propping her make-up mirror on the urinal.

'So am I. I hope it's not going to be too heavy for them.'

'It'll be lovely not to have to pong it, like we have to do for the kids.'

'Careful! It's going to flush!' The automatic flushing in gentlemen's conveniences can take a lady by surprise. Sue snatched her mirror in the nick of time.

It was a magical evening. The relationship between performer and audience is what makes the theatre the most exciting medium for actors. If they respond, you blossom, and that night all the barriers fell. It was like first love, tender and thrilling and genuinely high-tragic.

Live theatre rarely reaches Enugu. 'Mouldy porridge is better than nothing if you're starving,' I said to Sue as we peeled off our costumes, but I knew we had no cause to feel apologetic.

The air was thick with compliments, and our farewell party was properly joyous and emotional. Actors' emotions are close to the surface, which I'm certain is 'cause' and not 'effect', exposing our profession to accusations of insincerity off-stage. We live in the eye of an emotional cyclone, nightly suffering and rejoicing for our living, regularly going through the anxiety and elation of first nights, the despair of bad reviews, the blank hopelessness of being out of work. Though our emotions may be mercurial or ephemeral, they are sincere. And who wants to be well-balanced?

The revelry extended into the small hours, with talk of Ethiopia and Peru and the Falkland Islands, of Chaka Zulu and his barefoot warriors, and of the whites in Southern Africa who would rather see their children die than change. We discussed God and consenting adults and the International Monetary Fund, and fell into bed at 4 a.m. blissfully at peace, and I slept without nightmares, even though we were flying to Lagos in the morning.

Chapter Five

Beleaguered

A dribble of saliva stained the mat at our feet. The plump bottom was red with dust from the trucks that passed in the road only a sewer's distance away from the soles of the tiny feet. A fly landed on the stain and buzzed up round the baby's mouth, but he remained fast asleep. We slugged contentedly at warm Star from the bottle, and marvelled at how happily we had adjusted in four weeks to our itinerant life.

We were now in Yoruba country – different tribe, different language – and, if the driver who had met us at Lagos airport was typical of his people, we had nothing to fear. He was called Filament, and with our customary wit and originality we privately christened him 'The Watt?'

I am convinced that the name of a child influences his view of himself. Imaginative names are chosen by imaginative parents, of course, and an unusual environment is likely to produce an unusual personality. (*Pace* Paraffin Sandwich!) With a luminous name like Filament, how could he fail to want to shine among his fellows? He turned out to be mother, mentor, and Florence Nightingale to us, though he looked like Clement Attlee rolled out thin and covered in bitter chocolate.

Through miles of rubber plantations growing in regular glades, each tree inclining at a uniform angle away from the prevailing wind and carrying its own little pot at waist level, we drove towards Ibadan, the biggest Black City in Africa, where we were to spend the first night with Gordon and Julia Turner, the British Council rep. and his wife.

Their house left nothing to be desired. After discussing plans for the next two weeks over dinner, candle-lit for preference and not from necessity, Sue and I adjourned to our separate bedrooms in the confident expectation of passing a peaceful night.

Around that hour midway between retiring and the rising of the sun, when Death culls the dying like a patient panther, and Sleep finally relents and wraps the weary in his blessed mantle, a bomb went off in my knickers. Or so it seemed. To be awakened by such an explosion at that hour in the middle of Africa over-stimulates the imagination. I leapt out of bed and sprinted along the corridor to Sue's bedroom, my bare feet applauding on the cool terrazzo.

Sue was sitting up in bed with a look I can only describe as demented on her face.

'What the Hell was that?'

'Do you think we're being attacked?'

We heard shouts from the direction of the hall. Grabbing a towel for decency's sake from the back of a chair, I tiptoed with my heart buffeting my ribs towards the voices.

Gordon was standing in his pyjamas by the barely open door with a shot-gun in his hand, bellowing through the chained chink at the attacker beyond, whose shadow loomed menacingly through the opaque glass.

'You've *killed* him!' he was shouting.

'*Killed* him? Who was it for Christ's sake?'

Julia came running down the stairs carrying their six-year-old son who was wailing like a banshee in one arm, and a baseball bat in the other.

The voice outside babbled incomprehensibly.

'Hush, darling! What's happened?' Julia asked. 'Denis!' She shouted through the crack. 'Denis! Are you all right?'

There were further gusts of gibberish which our ears were not attuned enough to African tones to decipher.

'Let him in, darling. He's in a dreadful state.'

'*Denis!*' Gordon delivered a verbal slap as the voice beyond the door mounted towards hysteria. 'You'd better ring the police,' he said aside to his wife, as he cautiously unhooked the chain and opened the door. He briefly scanned the garden for any sign of a body or a wounded man in flight.

Across the threshold staggered a grizzled old tramp – Denis, the night-watchman – and in this Equatorial climate he was dressed for Siberia. A shapeless navy-blue great-coat patched with leather; a darned woollen cap pulled down over his tattered ears, which had been stretched into wide loops, though they were now innocent of any ornament; and in his mittened, quivering fingers shook a weapon that appeared to have been put together out of cocoa-tins – a rickety, rattling blunderbuss that looked far more lethal for the bearer than for the target.

'Sit down!' Gordon commanded, relieving Denis of the firearm, and the old man crumpled in a chair, rocking his head in his hands and keening in wordless distress. 'Fetch him a brandy, John. In the cupboard over there. What have you done with him? Denis! Where's the man you killed! Are you sure he's dead?'

'This weren't no man, boss. No sir. Denis is not scared of no man. Dis ting here was a WITCH! Let de ju-ju doctor dwindle me or put me in de grave, dis were a WITCH if ever I seen one. Oooh, mandakulu! Kulu mazie jokwu...' he moaned, or words to that effect, and the whites of his old eyes showed yellow and veiny.

'Denis!'

'Yes, boss. It come down out of nowhere, and is sitting on de fence by de garage gate – just where Master Andrew buried his dog Joley last week – it come out of de sky and is sittin' on de fence, and it fix me, boss – it fix me with de evil eye. Its eyes was red, boss. Red, RED, like burnin' fires, and dey fix me, so Denis can't move.'

'Hold it!' Gordon threw over his shoulder to Julia who had succeeded in contacting the police. 'False alarm!'

'It was probably an owl, Denis, don't you see that?'

'Denis has seen plenty of owls, boss. I been a night-watchman now five years. Dis weren't no owl. He was big like a man, and his wings was as long as a coffin. I don't know how Denis is liftin' de gun to 'is shoulder, with dese red eyes burnin' right through me – but de spirits are comin' to help Denis – Denis is a good man, boss – I never do no harm to no one – I get de gun up, and

I'm pointin' it right at his chest and I pullin' de trigger, and BANG! de witch is gone – GONE – and dere's goodness in de air!'

By torchlight we searched the garden. There was no dead bird, no blood, no feathers. Some lead shot was embedded in the fence just where Denis had indicated. But there were deep scratch marks in the hard earth over the Labrador's grave.

Perhaps Denis had seen a hungry vulture with insomnia. Perhaps the whole incident was an invention to gain a reward for saving us from the evil eye that burns like fire. Probably he imagined it. But Denis will affirm to his dying day that he saw a witch.

*

In the morning Sue's glands were swollen and she could hardly speak. Gordon whisked her to the doctor, where she was given a massive injection that made her squeak and a jar of two-toned anti-biotic capsules the size of jumping beans. But there was nothing else for it, I had to do the show on my own.

I was changing in a passage behind the stage in the altogether (these tights were a mistake), when a vibrating flurry of activity on my left calf made me suddenly aware that an enormous flame-lizard, with a purple body and a bulbous orange face, had mistaken me for a tree. I failed to keep my head. In fact, I almost broke it open on the pre-stressed concrete six feet above me.

My cries were answered by a thundering crowd of heavily nubile young ladies, late-arrivals from a school some sixty miles away, whose intention, it transpired, was not to rescue me from the lizard, but to grab at a pile of chairs behind me, which had served till that moment as a rack for my trousers. While I modestly clutched my groin and backed against the wall, the chairs flew past my head, spiky metal legs missing my eye and ear-apertures by a miracle, while all the girls, with unimpeachable good manners, entirely ignored an expanse of etiolated flesh, such as – one feels fairly confident in assuming – had been for the very first time exposed to their view.

I knew our programme by heart, but being neither an impersonator nor a ventriloquist doing the *Macbeth* duologues on my own presented problems, though playing Bassanio, Shylock *and*

Portia became rather exhilarating, even if the result owed a bigger debt to Monty Python than to the Bard.

Megalomania got me through, however, coupled with that irresistible glow of self-satisfaction one experiences when 'saving the day'. I strained my voice, but I managed a modestly heroic smile as Gordon half-carried me to the car. We were no longer in the land of hyperbole that we had dwelt in briefly after our ecstatic performance in the courtyard in Enugu under the stars.

'It was better than nothing,' he said, as he chucked me into the back seat.

Julia had taken Sue to the hospital again as her condition was deteriorating, where she had received yet another injection, but when we returned from the school she was crouched over the pan in the bathroom retching convulsively and shivering like a fern. I joined her on the cold tiles, but there was nothing anyone could do to relieve her acute distress. I have never felt further from home and the National Health Service. There are so many obscure diseases in 'The White Man's Grave' that we were all seriously alarmed.

A third doctor was summoned, a garrulous Indian lady in a chiffon sari who diagnosed malaria. She administered the quinine-based antidote, and within an hour the vomiting mercifully stopped though Sue was utterly exhausted and running with sweat. (A doctor in England later assured Sue that her symptoms did not indicate malaria – shivering, certainly, but not swollen glands and gastric disturbance. How, then, did the anti-malaria injection prove effective at once? Though we had religiously taken our weekly prophylactic pill, in constantly travelling we were at greater risk, for the strain of the disease, which is carried by the female mosquito, varies considerably over even quite short distances, and our pill was held to be right for some areas, but wrong for others.) Soon she was sleeping, though even in sleep she looked dejected.

Julia auditioned for Portia. She had taught the play at university, and she read the trial scene intelligently with the right stresses, so I gratefully gave her the part. It was no mean feat for a shy woman with no professional experience to face a thousand rowdy children for her acting debut, but she acquitted herself well, and both she and Gordon, who were intellectuals par excellence, were of invaluable assistance at question time.

*

'Backgammon?' I asked, as Sue slurped her consommé. 'Seeing as you're queer and in bed under the doctor, I'll let you win.'

'Like you did the last twice, you mean?'

'My mind wasn't on it.'

'I've never seen such concentration! If Denis had potted a *coven* of witches you wouldn't have turned a hair. The one on the top, I mean,' she added superfluously, referring to my intellectual brow.

'You're getting better all right. I could never understand till this moment why rudeness and health should go together.'

I took the tray and puffed up her pillows. There was a knock on the door and Filament stood in the corridor, his moustache just visible above an armful of scented magnolia.

'Get well soon,' he said.

*

We had to delay our departure 'on the road', for Sue, although making a splendid recovery, was still very weak. I took the opportunity to have two shirts made, as the ones I had brought from England had rotted with sweat. I bought a length of black material in the market to replace my Lebanese Abaya which was woolly and brought me out in a rash. Some mentholated powder alleviated the prickly-heat, some fungicidal ointment brought my Dobie's itch to its knees, a tin of Meggezones and a few days' rest revived my jaded vocal chords, so that I felt I was in fair repair for the weeks that lay ahead with my bravely determined fellow artiste.

*

Yorubas are less volatile than Ibos, and among them English is not so widely or so well spoken. Our first performance outside Ibadan, though well attended, was less of a party than a wake. We did shortened versions of both plays, which was as much as Sue could totter through, and no one stayed behind to ask a question. You can't win 'em all. But Filament had a cold-box waiting for us in the wings, full of iced beer and coca-cola – with the tops off! – which considerably raised our spirits.

Adeola may have been a splendid nurse, but she was a rotten hostess. The 'chop' was fine, but the evening was marred by her constant badgering of Wagie, her husband, who had suffered a stroke and was paralysed down one side. He had lost the use of his right arm, but he limped round the guests pouring out beer with his left, and offering groundnuts and spicy morsels with the best will in the world. Any illusions that the African wife is downtrodden was dispelled by the sorry spectacle of her insensitive behaviour.

'Wagie! Stow these things away! Nobody wants to see your daubings and scribbles! They know a real artist when they see one.'

For Wagie was a painter, and he was proudly producing assorted pieces of cardboard covered in images of unrelieved banality for our approval. They were bland and inept, without even the virtue of ethnic vision or naiveté, for he undoubtedly had a dogged, derivative technique, but it was difficult to find words of praise.

He had conquered his disability by training his left hand to substitute for his right, and what we wanted to say was, 'Any picture at *all* is a triumph, Wagie', but he wished to be judged by higher standards.

While slopping beer with his unpractised arm he had not stinted his own intake. He sat with eyebrows raised at his wife and the alien world, sloshed as a pixie. Since Filament had gone off for the evening, Wagie offered to drive us to our lodging at the school, and though we had qualms we had no alternative. Since he was not only paralysed but by this time paralytic, the short journey was unrelaxing. In this land of tropical rains and deep conduits, heading straight for right-angled bends or veering towards verges while in the erratic control of a drunken driver whose hand has to leave the wheel to change gear kept any inclination to doze off at bay.

*

After breakfast by an empty swimming-pool, swarming with colonies of lizards of the type that had familiarly assaulted me, scuttling and freezing by turns, then dipping their orange heads like those horrible toy-dogs people put in the rear-windows of their cars, we drove for hours to Ilesha, and gave a dusty, dull performance. We ate corned-beef and hard-boiled eggs from our cold-box, sitting on the floor of a Volunteer's flat, a freckled, irrepressible lass from Kirkcudbright who was the only European for miles around. Her infatuation with this unspectacular town in Nigeria was total. Her spirits were so high that in the silences in our conversation they would burst forth in snatches of virtuoso whistling, loud and tremulous as a musical saw. She had two rabid Alsatians, a Harley-Davidson motor-bike, and an adopted chocolate eclair called Yummy, who was at two and a half years old already a chronic cuddle-a-holic. I suspect my beard aggravated his addiction, for all during lunch his chubby arms never left my neck, and he was quite unconcerned that his crinkles got covered in crumbs.

By the end of the afternoon performance we began to get the measure of our Yoruba audiences. It was not that they were uninterested or bored, they simply made less display of their feelings than the Ibos, and their questions revealed a realistic approach to life. 'Where's the rest of the company?', and 'What are Shakespeare's qualifications?' Yorubas were also more reticent about inviting us to share their homes, so that in the Western State we spent more time in Rest-Houses than with families.

The salty soup, chicken and chips, and pancake with disinfectant filling were served by the unsmiling proprietrix of the Rest-House at Oyo, who was imprisoned in an ocean of fat, with tides and currents and heavy seas plunging and swirling beneath her gown as she walked. Over a pot of tea, to say she unbent would be exaggerating, but she engulfed the chair next to Sue and painstakingly taught her the game of Ayo, played on a board with hollowed-out cups containing large seeds or cowrie shells. Sue had to teach it to me later, as I couldn't concentrate on the lady's instructions for watching the ebb and flow of her gargantuan bosom, and the nodular wobble of her arms like thighs.

It was a comfortable, colonial type of establishment, and a fan revolved above my bed which gave me nightmares. Fans and air-conditioning I find singularly unsoporific. My dreams become obsessively peripatetic. I am always en route to somewhere, usually unpleasant. Sue on the other hand will put up with anything to keep cool, and it would take gun-fire to wake her with her good ear in the pillow. But this fan rattled and shook in such an unpredictable series of frenzied climaxes, interspersed with periods of relative calm to lull one into a state of false security, that I was certain it was going to fly off its spindle in the small hours and chop me to bits. It was scant comfort that just along the road was the best Maternity Hospital in the Western State, so I rose when I estimated that Sue was soundly sleeping and switched it off.

As it swung into silence there was an audible plop on my bed. Audible plops in the night in tropical countries strike terror to the heart of the chicken-livered like me. With a fine disregard for my sleeping colleague, I turned on the light. It was not very big, and I had no idea whether it was dangerous, but lying on the very spot which I had vacated only a moment before lay what can only be described as a snake. It was black, about a foot long, with a little triangular head, and it meandered insolently across the crumpled sheet and slid to the floor. There is something which soldiers experience in battle which is not courage, but closer to its opposite. Nevertheless it spurs one to action. Before Sue could draw breath to complain about my disturbing her night's rest, I was hammering at the beastly reptile with my left Macbeth boot like a man possessed. By the time Sue had flung back her mosquito net and opened her mouth to scream, there was nothing but a pulpy bloody mess on the quarry-tiles and I was quivering with shock. In the morning Filament identified the skin as that of a baby black mamba, whose baby-bite, notwithstanding, is fatal.

*

On Friday the Thirteenth of February there was nothing on the radio but martial music, which to countries familiar with such happenings is a sure sign that there has been 'a coup'. There were battalions of soldiers on the road to our first school, but they seemed unconcerned, and among the staff and pupils, who were as ignorant of what had happened as we, there was an expectant, almost festive atmosphere. It vanished when we heard the news.

The President of the Military Government, Lieutenant General Muritala Mohammed, had been assassinated. On his way to Government House his limousine had been ambushed and sprayed with machine-gun bullets. No one knew how many had died, but a high-ranking officer in the army, Colonel Dimka, broke the radio silence with the announcement that he had now taken over the government of the country, in such a way that made it clear that he was the instigator of 'the coup' and directly responsible for Mohammed's murder. Dimka's brother-in-law, the ex-President Gowon of Nigeria, is studying at Warwick University in England. We had no idea at that time how tragic would be the results of this family connection.

Both Gowon and Dimka come from a small tribe called the Tiv, but the majority of the population of Nigeria belongs to one of the three major tribes, Hausa in the North, Ibo in the East, and Yoruba in the West, and each can barely tolerate the other two. It says much for Muritala Mohammed that, though he was a Hausa, his death was mourned equally by Ibos and Yorubas.

A curfew was imposed from 6 p.m. till 6 a.m., so that our afternoon performances had to be cancelled, as outlying schools would have been unable to return to their compounds in time. This unexpected leisure gave us the opportunity to meet two of the most extraordinary people I have met in my life.

The first was Twins 77. That's his name. Pronounced Twins Seven Seven. We were told that his mother had borne six children before the advent of Twins and his brother and that they had all died. He is Nigeria's best-known artist, and is justly famous.

We were browsing in his shop-cum-showroom waiting for his arrival. He sometimes paints on beaten tin or aluminium, frequently combining paint with beads and seeds and shells, and the effect is startling, original, and inimitably African. He also paints with inks on cloth, which he prefers to do lying full length on the floor so that he can sleep when he feels like it. In one such painting which he had been working on, he later pointed out the blot he had made when it was announced on the radio that the president had been assassinated. Filament told us that Twins had recently returned from a trip to America, where his pictures fetch a high price, with one of his eight wives, an artist in her own right who specialises in batiks. He is also a composer and a musician, with his own group, his own recording company, and his own extremely prosperous nightclub.

As we were admiring his work he came in dripping from the shower, clad only in a towel. His hair was knotted in a score of little ribbons, and his cheeks were deeply furrowed with tribal scars. He was about thirty, almost vulgarly handsome, and flagrantly charming. He immediately invited us up to his bedroom.

He led the way across the yard past a lean-to garage that housed his petunia-pink Cadillac with telephone and TV installed, through a family of chickens that were scratching in a pile of refuse round a life-sized fairground figure, and up an outside staircase to his boudoir.

It was full. Several men in baggy pyjamas and embroidered caps lounged on the floor against one wall. The king-sized bed was unmade, and a young girl was attempting to iron on it, while another, heavily pregnant, got in the way. The stereo recordplayer was thumping out one of Twins' heavy rock compositions, and an elderly lady with a smouldering fag stuck to her pendulous lower lip stood in the middle of the room waggling her bottom to the music and swinging her handbag with one hand, while, for no clear reason, ringing a little brass bell with the other. Twins introduced her as a High Priestess of the Oshun Grove but she carried on dancing. There was a very large television set in a corner with a tangerine-coloured telephone on the top, and

a portable set in another, beside a second telephone which was knicker-pink. Twins managed to speak at length into both these intruments, despite the noise, before settling himself on the bed between the thighs of another wife who had arrived bearing a comb with teeth like a cross-grained saw to tease his ribboned knots into a frothy halo. Filament muttered to us with amusement, but no disapproval, that it was unusual for men to resort to this hair-knotting device.

Some other wives brought bottles of beer and bowls of nuts and albums of photographs for us to peruse. Twins at Niagara Falls. Twins with his latest L.P. Twins opening his exhibition in New York. Twins with his wives and some of his children. Twins in his nightclub dancing 'The Highlife'.

His coiffeur complete, the wives on the bed helped him into an immaculate white suit, and, while the priestess rang her bell at me and dragged me up to dance, Twins donned his jewellery, most of which he had fashioned himself. Strings of heavy necklaces and bangles of jade and cufflinks of carbuncle and several outsize rings on every finger. All in white, scarred and primped and decorated like a Christmas tree, he was a veritable African Liberace.

We descended the stairs to have a photograph taken in front of a shrine to Ogun, the God of Iron.

'I'm coming to your show, Suzan,' Twins said decisively, 'if you'll let me. I know it's Shakespeare, but he's peanuts to an intellectual like me.' He yodelled with that infectious brand of laughter which is impossible for Europeans to emulate.

'It's for children, Twins, and I assure you we look pretty dowdy compared with you.'

He yelped and did a little dance, rattling his bangles about his ears.

'Why don't you stay on a couple of days, and come to my nightclub? I'll give you the time of your life.'

The club opened only at weekends.

We sadly shook our heads. 'Off to Ife tomorrow.'

After much hugging and back-slapping and holding of hands, we took our leave. The priestess rang her bell and delivered a long prayer in Yoruba, while at the same time, naturally, swivelling her hips. We were touched by her concern, till she demanded with menaces to be paid.

'What do you think he gets up as on special occasions?' Sue asked, as we skimmed along a good road to our Rest-House in Oshogbo.

'There goes a truly fulfilled man,' I said, half in earnest.

'Irresistible…and not short on ego.'

'And doesn't he enjoy it!'

*

At the following morning's performance our generalisations about Yorubas were knocked on the head. The children were noisily appreciative. They muttered 'The quality of mercy...' along with Sue, and cheered when she 'pulled the rabbit out of the hat' – 'Take thou no jot of blood!' Twins arrived late with an entourage, and joined in the general rejoicing. Though faint and sodden at the end we were euphoric, and Filament, who watched our every show with critical intensity, fed us a few sparing words of praise along with our cold beer.

After question-time, the bespectacled principal made a speech of thanks, though not a word was heard above the uproar.

'They were relatively quiet for us, which proves something!' Sue whispered.

The principles then graciously presented us with a packet of biscuits each. My 'thank-yous' being lost in the din, one thousand kids went barmy as I got carried away and kissed her hand.

After lunch with Twins, and a fond farewell, we drove past stalls along the road selling bottles of distilled palm-wine, or 'Kai-Kai', with imaginative and poetic names in Yoruba. 'A bottle of "Drink-too-much-and-go-blind" please.' Or 'Two bottles of "Great-big-kick-up-the-arse". '

Having the rest of the day to ourselves, we decided to go in search of the legendary High Priestess of Obatala.

This amazing woman had been a young sculptress of some reputation working in Vienna. Her name is Susan Wenger. Just after the Second World War she visited Nigeria, fell in love with the Yoruba culture, and has been in Oshogbo ever since. To learn the Yoruba language is a feat which very few Europeans ever attempt. It is tonal, which means that the same sequence of vowels and consonants can have as many as six or seven utterly diverse meanings, depending on how the word is inflected, or 'sung'. She not only speaks it like a native, she has immersed herself totally in their alien, animistic, pagan beliefs, and has been appointed by the Yorubas themselves the White High Priestess of Obatala and the Oshun Grove. She has restored her goddess's shrine in the forest, adding concrete to the traditional mud of the 'buildings' and 'sculpture', so that they will endure through the mighty rains. Apart from the savage originality of her own work, she has trained local artisans – bricklayers and the like – to give full play to their indigenous folk imagination, producing an explosion of ethnic art which has made her celebrated throughout the world.

We had been warned that she was formidable, and sometimes ferocious if crossed in argument by sceptics. She is also something of a recluse, and wary of visiting Europeans. Sue and I hoped, however, that as actors she might consider us to be part of the artist's lunatic fringe, and less likely to be antagonistic to her bizarre beliefs.

We asked a young man the way to her house, but he scuttled off without a word, his eyes rolling. It was as if we had been in Transylvania and had asked to be directed to Castle Dracula. We found it eventually, a tall, four-storey building, Portuguese returned-slave architecture, Gothic and rambling, with the terraces on the top floor caged in for her monkeys. Leading up to the front door there was a sweeping balustrade, voluptuously ornate, composed of human and animal and organic forms, rounded and asymmetrical, reminiscent, in a sense, of Gaudi. The whole house was smothered in a canopy of bougainvillea, making it a scarlet oasis in the rust-red dust and iron-roofed ramshackle bustle of Oshogbo.

Our knocking was answered by an assorted giggle of half-naked children, clamouring and jostling and behaving altogether in a reprehensibly unsinister manner. Using Filament as an interpreter, we asked politely if Miss Wenger was at home, and whether she would receive two travelling English actors. At this, their hilarity stopped some passers-by, but they raced indoors, falling over each other and yelling, while we fried patiently on the doorstep. Filament explained that the children were *probably* not all hers, as she had a reputation for collecting waifs, both human and animal. She was in, and had agreed to meet us.

We sidled nervously into the gloom. The children gambolled about us as we climbed a narrow wooden staircase up two floors into a tiny room filled to overflowing with carvings covered in dust: grotesque and violent figures with bulging eyes and jutting breasts and cone-like penises, some with 'hair' of cowrie shells (used as money in the old days), rocking-horses like demons with phallic tongues obscenely protruding from leering mouths. We were invited to sit, to our surprise, on pieces of bronze sculpture that bore no resemblance to chairs, and which turned out, naturally, to be fiercely uncomfortable, and we were joined by several slightly mangy dogs who gave us a disdainful sniff-over.

We heard a woman's pleasant voice raised, but not in anger, and the children's shouting instantly subsided. Susan Wenger slowly came into the room without a smile, her wide-set pale-blue eyes staring with defensive intensity. She was a strikingly handsome woman of about sixty. (From the evidence of early photographs published recently in a book about her work, she was undoubtedly a great beauty.) She had short, still blonde hair, and she was wearing, which was a surprise and perhaps a disappointment, a neat summer frock. In fluent English, with a strong German accent, she said, 'Please sit down. It is kind of you to visit me. I see so few people from Europe...it is a pleasure. You are welcome. So. You are *actors*? How interesting.'

She sat on another piece of metal sculpture by the door (there was no more space in the room), leaning against the lintel and gently caressing her dogs, picking out ticks with bright-green fingers laden with rings. I thought the colour must be verdigris from her brass and copper jewellery, but later we learned it was from the dye which she uses to make batiks. When she saw that we were friendly, she blossomed. She was urbane and intelligent and far from mad. She held court, of course, but not about herself, to our chagrin, but about Shakespeare and art as a means of communication.

She refuted the suggestion that Shakespeare might be irrelevant to Africans.

'Even if he were, which he isn't, he is relevant to the English, and you are showing us your greatest poet.'

She indicated her roomful of macabre figures.

'This may not be relevant to the English, but you are interested, yes? And it helps you to understand us, perhaps. I am all for cultural exchange, without proselytising...'

We shared her detestation of missionary zeal. We would rather learn of other people's beliefs than impose our own upon them. Though few people would venture as far from home along that road as Susan Wenger.

She declined to accompany us to her Grove in the forest, though before we left, she showed us a photograph of herself officiating at the annual festival in honour of the goddess whom she served. She was standing surrounded by black priestesses with a crowd of many thousands receding in the background. She was dressed from head to foot in white robes adorned with a single necklace from which was suspended a monkey's skull. Her hands were raised, and her eyes blazed with a fanatical fire that has given birth to a legend as powerful as one from the pages of Rider Haggard.

The gate to the Grove was a monumental mud-red maw, gaping six feet above our heads as we passed through its gorge into the sanctuary beyond.

Primitive, heroic-sized creatures, weathered and devilish, lurked in the shadowy undergrowth between shrines with swooping thatch like great birds poised for flight. The central shrine, housing the blood-caked sacrificial altar, was on a smaller, human scale; each pillar that supported the roof was different and seemed to grow with a life of its own from the forest floor.

The Grove itself was peaceful and quite beautiful, a natural glade carpeted with crisp grey leaves, shaded by deciduous trees that seemed to touch the sky, and sloping gently to a pool in, the river where a sprinkling of scarlet petals sailed slowly by on their own reflections. If we did not feel the presence of the goddess, in contrast with the ghastly congestion of the town, we could not fail to rejoice in the beauty of primal nature.

Chapter Six

Besieged

Ife is the Mecca of Yoruba culture, and it boasts the biggest university in the world. The campus is on a Napoleonic scale, with splendid modern buildings, some still unfinished, laid out along miles of wide, tended avenues. The students in this prestigious seat of learning are the coming generation of leaders and professional men and they are a barometer of the political atmosphere of the country. They are aware that they are the young elite, and the novelty of wielding power sometimes leads them to abuse it.

There had been angry demonstrations in the wake of the president's assassination. The 'coup' had been abortive, the army was still in the command of Muritala Mohammed's supporters, and his murderer, Dimka, had disappeared. In the frustration of thwarted vengeance, and in the absence of any concrete evidence of how the plot against their leader's life had been engineered, the C.I.A., the organisation everyone loves to hate, was made the scapegoat, with the result that the American professor and his wife with whom we were lodging within the university grounds were jumpy, and with reason.

Students all over the world often confuse violence with idealism, and in Ife, with many whites on the teaching staff, racial antagonism adds fuel to the fire. A group of radicals brandishing clubs and machetes had already disrupted a predominantly white teachers' meeting, though no one had been hurt. As the curfew fell at six o'clock, the massive gates of this academic state within a state clanged shut, and we were locked in with two Americans among the largest population of angry students in Africa.

At about seven-thirty all the lights went out. We froze like lizards when you throw something at them. The boulevards and libraries and laboratories and lecture halls, the sports-fields and accommodation blocks, the Olympic pool and the Garden City of staff bungalows were all engulfed in a menacing black silence. We sat in the dark, afraid to light a candle, straining our ears for the sound of approaching feet.

'What was that?' hissed Sue, who was at a disadvantage with only one listening device.

A strangled shout floated on the wind out of the darkness from a long way off. It was followed several moments later by an angry babble, much nearer than before, which quickly formulated into a slogan chanted in unison. Our American professor rose and locked all the doors. 'C.I.A.!' I could pick out and that was all, but then I heard 'M.P.L.A.!' as well. We stood by the louvred glass windows looking helplessly out through the cracks as the shouting drew nearer. And nearer. Now we could see little points of light from hand-held electric torches, jogging up and down as their invisible bearers sprinted towards our house. The professor was a Catholic, and he prayed. They came closer, till we could see a kaleidoscopic snake of colour, jeans and shirts and robes, flickering in the bouncing beams, and the silhouette of its shadow was spiky with the weapons they were carrying.

Suddenly the procession was plunged into day-bright dazzling light. A convoy of cars, their headlamps blazing, squealed to a halt, and the colourful clothes of the students were blotted out by a wall of uniformed police. They carried guns and whips, but they did not use them, though the ensuing dialogue was long and ferocious.

At long last they dispersed, and the professor poured us all a large drink.

'I guess we're gonna be all right now,' he said, lighting some candles.

'We're supposed to be going to Folarin's for dinner. Do you think it'll be safe?' Sue asked.

'You'll be safer there than here. He's Yoruba and she's English. I should go, if I were you.'

'What about you? We don't like to leave you...'

'Oh, don't worry. Now they've let off some steam, I reckon things will cool down for a while. And the police are on the alert, so we should be O.K. Have a nice evening,' he said, as Filament swung the car into the drive.

*

We felt secure in the bosom of Folarin's family. Mags, his fine-boned aristocratic wife, and the mother of their three beautiful brown children, served goat for dinner, which was delicious, to a small cosmopolitan group composed of a Greek-American couple, several Nigerians, and a lady from Ceylon who liked to hold one's hand in conversation because she was blind. Folarin's designs for the Nottingham Playhouse productions of *Caligula* and *Tamburlaine* were vivid and barbaric, and, first seen that evening by candlelight with the sound of distant drums, the images have remained indelible. He is also a well-known painter and sculptor, and he was working on a commissioned head of the Shah's wife, Princess Farah Diba of Iran, which was striking because of its African treatment of a Caucasian face.

The drumming had started shortly after we arrived. In view of the scene we had witnessed earlier Sue and I were apprehensive, but the Nigerians present seemed unconcerned. The beat was different from the compulsive rhythms we had watched the Ibo virgins dance to in Mbaise. It started and stopped and was taken up again without a recognisable pattern.

'Listen to the drums!' Folarin held up his hand. 'Do you hear? They are talking to each other.'

'Is it like a sophisticated sort of morse-code?' I asked.

'Not at all. They are talking in Yoruba. Any Yoruba can understand the talking drums with practice, though only some can play them.'

'How can drums speak a language?'

'Not *any* language, but Yoruba, certainly, because it is tonal. The notes and stresses can be easily reproduced. If you listen to the wireless, you'll hear the call-sign for N.B.S., which is easily understood by every Yoruba, and it says on the drums, 'Good-morning, Ladies and Gentlemen. This is the Nigerian Broadcasting Service.'

Wondering what messages were pulsing through the air at this time of crisis, I said, 'It's a good way of cutting the 'phone bills.'

The electricity remained off all through the night, but the throbbing drums seemed to purge the violence in the air, and when they finally stopped the silence was somehow no longer threatening.

*

The museum at Ife is small but select, and the relics it contains are of a very unprimitive society. Highly sophisticated heads in bronze, the features indisputably African, but the workmanship reminiscent of Ancient Greece. The faces are often ribbed vertically, but in such regular furrows that they cannot be intended to represent tribal scars. When viewed from a distance, this ribbing seems to lend the heads an almost supernatural luminosity, which may be the reason for this weird device.

There is a squat little couple, also in bronze, which is delicately executed; it is both funny and touching, qualities rare in antiquities and absent in more recent African art. They are looking straight ahead, she hanging onto his arm like a dignified wife, but on closer inspection one naked foot is surreptitiously curled round her husband's ankle as though for comfort while posing for the artist. There was also a horse and rider in brass, so wild and original it was comparable to T'ang or Tutenkhamun in its evolved, decorative symbolism.

We were needlessly nervous of the performance at the university, for the lecture-hall was packed with friendly faces, and their questions at the end continued through the sandwich lunch they had provided for us. Everywhere students are so eager to learn, so disarmingly uncomplacent, that question-time became our favourite part of the programme when we didn't have to tear ourselves away for a second performance or a long drive.

Filament had blossomed into ethnic gear since we left Ibadan, his British Council uniform exchanged for swirling pink pyjamas, and the transformation was liberating. On the drive to Ondo he talked with pride of his wife and family, with regret of his lack of education, and, to our amazement, with humour of his conquest of alcoholism. Watching our show had whetted his interest in Shakespeare, and he had read both plays in their entirety.

'This dead butcher and his fiend-like queen...' he said, tutting and shaking his head. He went on to put up a cogent defence of Macbeth as a statesman in an age of violence, and of Lady Macbeth as a dutiful wife.

The discussion was in full spate when we came upon a crowd by the roadside, gathered round a cow which lay kicking and thrashing its tail with a fountain of blood issuing from its slashed throat. Abbatoirs exist in the cities, but in the country cattle are apparently slaughtered where they stand. A youth leapt out of the way of the dying animal's flailing hooves and thumped against the bonnet of the car as we passed. Filament drove on, though we were concerned to find out if the boy had been hurt.

'Never stop,' Filament warned us. 'If someone is hurt, it is always the driver's fault, and, black or white, you will be lynched and stoned to death. Just keep driving, that's the rule.'

A platoon of soldiers with rifles slung across their shoulders waved us down to a crawl, and for a moment it seemed that Birnam Wood had come to Dunsinane, for ahead of us was a Moving Grove. A large band of students, all carrying branches, with fillets of pampas grass tied round their foreheads, was marching six abreast in the middle of the road. Some carried placards: 'We are for the M.P.L.A.', 'Kill Dimka!', 'C.I.A. Go to Hell!', while others were shouting and beating on skin drums. Alongside ran children and supporters, so that to pass the demonstration was impossible. We had to suffocate for about a mile, as, on Filament's advice, we wound up the windows and locked the doors. There may have been no danger, but feelings run high on such occasions, and the glances we received from the army and the passing crowd were not friendly. The leafy boughs they carried were signs of mourning for Muritala Mohammed. Dimka, his murderer, who was still missing or dead, was accused in *The Times of Nigeria* of 'Vaulting Ambition'. When we did *Macbeth* after the assassination, there was no doubt of its relevance, and the atmosphere in our audiences was electric.

*

Romulus gulped at the warm milk in the eye-dropper, avidly kneading with his paws in Angela's lap. His glittering black eyes hardly flickered when the purring tabby put her feet up beside him and officiously washed his downy backside. Though the cat had accepted Romulus totally, along with her own kittens, she could not feed him, as pussy titty and genet snout do not correspond.

Besides the cat, her five kittens, and the adopted genet, Adam and Angela Farley kept a wiry-haired hound of mixed ancestry sanctimonious parrot called Willie who said grace before meals, and after and at any other time he felt religious, two miniature Bambis called 'Daika's' browsing on frangipani petals and assorted fruit, their tails whirling like paper-windmills, and a red patas monkey on a long string who lived up a capok tree, descending only to eat his bananas and to bite people.

Adam was a scientist and Angela a teacher, and, though they had no official connection with the British Council, through the camaraderie of the British in the Bush they had offered us lodgings while playing in the vicinity of Ondo. Their house stood on its own in the middle of the forest, in a garden bright with hibiscus and Pride of Barbados and white star-like jasmine. When the waxy, insect-eating plants by the front door twitched, the dog barked. There were two stewards called Christian and Cosmos which seemed propitious, and our hosts were as kind to humans as they were to animals. They could hardly be blamed for the misfortunes that lay in store.

If there was an Accident-Prone Competition Sue would incontestably emerge Miss World. The tabby nurtured her brood in a box under the stair, kittens and adopted genet wobbling together around her on unsteady legs, their tails borne aloft like fluffy banners, viewing their tiny world with that look of startled seriousness so irresistible to the sentimental. Before sitting down to breakfast Sue gurgled over them for ten minutes, as I admit I had done before her, then she stood up and knocked herself out on the supporting beam. Almost. She had a lump on her forehead the size of a pigeon's egg. But she managed to force down some toast and marmalade before returning to her room to swish through her lingerie.

While I brought my diary up to date, she pottered out, still in her nightie, to hang it on the line. The early morning dew was cool between her toes, and the heady scent of jasmine hung over the garden. Pastel-blue wax-bills and iridescent sun-birds bathed,

twittering on the lawn. She hummed a snatch of 'Fee-lings', and forgot the throbbing bump on her brow. A spine-chilling shriek brought us all running, Angela and Christian and Cosmos and me. Sue was sprawled full-length on the ground, slithering and skidding on the wet grass, scrabbling frantically to get out of reach of the red patas monkey who had leapt from his capok tree, snatched her dripping underwear like a crazed fetishist and brought her down with a flying tackle. He stood on his hind legs at the end of his rope, chattering insanely through bared teeth, and from time to time he took a vicious bite in displacement aggression at a pair of Sue's freshly laundered drawers.

She was suffering from shock and a few scratches, but was miraculously unbitten.

'Well, at least nothing much worse can happen,' she said, fingering her lump, and dabbing at her lacerated arm with T.C.P.

But she was wrong.

✻

The children were studying *Macbeth* and *The Merchant* as part of their curriculum, and they wanted, above all, to pass their exams. Where there are eight hundred applicants for eighty places in a school, paramount importance attaches to winning certificates. Without the proof of it, education is worthless. More and more, our audience asked us 'exam' questions, wanting the 'right' answer. Two molecules of hydrogen combine with one molecule of oxygen to form water. That is a fact. But in literature and the arts, where the study is life, and the subject is as complex as people, one can discuss, offer an opinion, agree or disagree, but one cannot give the kind of 'correct' answer they were hoping for.

'Does Shylock deserve his punishment?'

'Who was more responsible for Duncan's murder, Macbeth or his wife?'

'Is Bassanio an unscrupulous fortune-hunter?'

They took our open-ended replies with good grace, but I suspect they thought we were purposely evasive.

✻

Willie was croaking grace when we got home, but Adam said it again before dinner. The parrot took umbrage in such a strong Yoruba accent that we couldn't understand him, so Angela put the cover over his cage which shut him up like magic.

My mouth was full of avocado when I felt a sharp stab on my big toe. I cursed under my breath that I had changed from my desert boots to flip-flops for comfort. Everything that creeps and flies seems to bite in this part of Africa, and I wanted to stamp the wretched parasite underfoot, but I could see nothing except my pink swelling toe when I searched under the table.

Cosmos was serving the lemon mousse when Christian burst in from the kitchen.

'I think we have some trouble sir,' he said to Adam in a voice too calm to be comforting.

'What's wrong?' Adam asked.

'Ants,' was all he said, and I went on eating till I saw that the colour had drained from Angela's face.

Without a word, Adam rose from the table and we followed him into the kitchen.

From the windowsill, down the wall and across the floor was a faint, shimmering smear about a foot wide, which disappeared under the larder door. Each ant was almost an inch long, but the numbers of which the trail was composed relegated the individual to an insignificant part of a relentless whole which moved in a curving sweep across the vinyl tiles. The sill was wet with insecticide, and as if mocking the efforts to deter it the procession swarmed over the empty cannisters which had been discarded in its path.

Angela ran to the larder and opened the door. The shelves looked as if lumpy treacle had been poured all over them. There was no shape to the neat piles of tins and sealed containers in which a careful housewife in Africa stores food, but the crumbs and specks which may be invisible to the human eye were enough to attract the insects' attention. For the moment.

Adam ran to the garage and returned with a can of petrol. Regardless of the herbaceous border and the flowering shrubs, he drenched the ants outside the window in a torrent of it. They seemed to disperse a little, floundering in the pungent fuel, but then they converged again out of the darkness in even greater numbers, and continued on exactly the same path up the outside wall to the window, though the smear now seemed darker and wider. Throwing caution to the winds, he shouted at us all to keep clear. With reckless courage he threw a lighted match onto the patch of dark earth where he had emptied the can, but it blew out before it landed. He tried again. And again. But the parched earth had soaked up the petrol immediately, and all he could raise was a small burst of flame which died even as it ignited. Cosmos appeared with some paraffin, with which we had more success. We lit a barrier of fire across the advancing column, and though hundreds of the creatures plunged into it and sizzled, a squirming

hill of them piled up on the far side as the vanguard turned back
on the advancing army.

While Adam attended to the fire, we returned to the kitchen.
Angela and Christian were knocking the tins off the shelves in
the larder into plastic bags, and throwing them, still swarming
with the tenacious insects, out into the garden. Another sharp
stab on my toe was the reminder I needed to charge upstairs and
change into my boots.

Sue was wielding a broom when I returned, sweeping wriggling
mounds out the back door, while individual ants swarmed over
the head of the broom and scuttled up the handle. With a dish-
cloth she flicked them off between strokes. There was still a mass
of insects everywhere, but they were no longer in an organised
column. With a feeling of the utmost relief, we realised we had
routed them.

Then we heard the dog squeal. It was a continuous, terrified
yelp of pain. Adam reached him first. He was chained up for the
night by the front door, and already his paws were crawling with
ants. Adam loosed him from his chain, and he cavorted on the
spot, whimpering pathetically and snapping savagely at his own
feet. There was no time to go to his aid, for while we had diverted
the column from the rear part of the house it had reformed, and
was now pouring through the front door in a river four feet
across and inches deep in layer upon layer of slithering insects.
Like molten metal or black lava it slid sluggishly, inexorably forward, invading the house with no possibility now of stopping
it. We were struck quite powerless with horror.

'The kittens!' Angela gasped. We ran back through the kitchen
to the box under the stairs. The cat was standing, her striped fur
on end, snarling and spitting at the millions upon millions of ants
as they passed within feet of her 'lair'.

'There are only two here!' Angela cried. The genet and three
others had gone. The tabby jumped into the box, seized one of
the two remaining kittens by the neck in a ferocious bite, and
leapt onto the fourth step of the open staircase, banging the kitten's
bottom on every tread all the way to the top.

'She's moved them!' Angela groaned with relief. 'I hope to
goodness they'll be safe.'

For we could not ascend the stair to ascertain their whereabouts without crunching through the loathsome flood that still poured like vengeance through the house. We put the last kitten on the stair when the cat returned, and joined Adam outside, who was standing disconsolate in a group with Christian's wife and two children, whom the steward had collected from his house at the end of the garden. No one knew in which direction this monstrous phenomenon would flow, so Christian was taking no chances.

'There's nothing we can do,' Adam said, 'except wait.' But the advancing column receded as far as one could see into the darkness, and he told us they frequently stretch for miles.

We collected the dog, whose paws were raw and bleeding. We piled into two cars and drove to a neighbour's house, whose children were at school in the U.K., so they had rooms for us all, though none of us slept a wink.

In the morning we returned to a desolate scene. The kitchen was more or less as we had left it, and upstairs was untouched. The food on the dining-table had all gone, however, and the plates were grimy with the insects' excreta. A few half-eaten dead ants lay crinkled in the sticky wake of the army's passage. The curtains were tattered round the edges, and three limp pieces of string were all that remained of the candles.

With an intake of breath, Angela whipped the cover off the parrot. Willie had said his last grace, for all that remained of him was a pile of green feathers and a skeleton picked clean on the bottom of his cage.

※

In the newspapers and on the radio, the blame for conspiring with the revolutionary group in the army who had attempted the 'coup' was lifted from the C.I.A., and placed squarely, though unfairly, on the British. 'BLOODY BLOODY PLOT!' was one headline, 'BRITISH HIGH COMMISSIONER IMPLICATED'.

After announcing the assassination of the president and declarin ghimself in power, Dimka had forced his way, accompanied by armed gunmen, into Sir Martin Le Quesne's office, and insisted on telephoning his (Dimka's) brother-in-law, the ex-President

Gowon, at Warwick. Allowing this conversation to take place was interpreted by the Nigerian Government as collusion on the part of the high commissioner, though, even if guns had not been used, how was Sir Martin Le Quesne to know that the 'coup' would be abortive and that Dimka was not the new president?

The media were now demanding the extradition of Gowon back to Nigeria, but what humane government, even if there had been evidence to support the contention that Gowon was a traitor to Nigeria and the inspiration behind Mohammed's murder, would deport a man to certain death by firing-squad?

There were rumours that Dimka's faction had been much more numerous than those now in power cared to admit, so that an outside scapegoat had to be found to divert attention from the deep divisions within the army. As the extradition of Gowon would have been the only act to placate the Nigerians, and since Her Majesty's Government refused to comply, overnight the Americans were exonerated, and the British had become enemy number one.

*

A bumper-to-bumper snake of traffic blocked the road on the way to our next performance at Akure.

Our new British Council 'protector' was a sad-eyed young Welshman called David who had cause to look sad, for his wife had recently lost her battle against mental illness and had thrown herself under a train. He was coping alone with the rearing of two children, the elder at school in England, the younger, while David was 'on the road', in the care of a nanny.

Glancing at our watches, we anxiously shifted our weight on the rumpled towels we were now in the habit of putting on the car-seats to absorb the sweat. As Dimka had still not been found, there were exhaustive police-checks on every major road.

Filament, muttering an expletive which was unlike him, took it on himself to pull out from behind the long line of stationary vehicles, and he sped down the middle of the road through a hail of abuse from the frustrated drivers towards the front of the queue.

A soldier brandishing a rifle, his torso coiled in bandoliers bristling with cartridges, whirled round upon our advancing car and slammed his fist on the bonnet. He was joined by another, who came running with the light of battle in his eye. They shouted and shook their guns at us, and their furious gestures indicated that they wished us to return and wait in line.

Filament, resplendent in his patterned pyjamas, jumped out, seizing his British Council badge from the dashboard, and engaged them in conversation. He spoke in English, which surprised us, but Filament knew somehow that the soldiers were Hausas, and they knew that he was Yoruba, and English was their only common language.

Filament explained without raising his voice that a thousand children were waiting for us, that we all had ample proof of identity, that the bags in our boot contained costumes and not guns, that none of us was Dimka in disguise or whited-up, and asked politely if we might pass. Their answer was to order us all immediately out of the car. They were in a highly excitable state and one of them kept slapping the butt of his rifle perilously near the trigger-guard; I simply prayed that the safety-catch was functioning and on.

An officer arrived, and they all fingered our passports gingerly. Though they were side by side, they shouted at each other in their own language. Not all Nigerians are as quietly reasonable as Filament.

'Go back to the end of the line!' the senior soldier barked, 'and wait your turn!'

There seemed nothing else for it, but Filament had another idea.

'I tell you what. I'll ask the first car you let through to take a message to Akure High to cancel the performance. Hundreds of children will be coming from Akure and from Ado Ikiti and from further than that hoping to learn something to help them pass their exams, but it can't be helped. Even education has to bow to authority. I'll park off the road, and we'll stay here with you tilt you decide to let us go.'

While they were still mulling over what he had said, he leap, into the car, swerved it round the barrier onto the dusty vergel while one soldier swung the muzzle of his rifle towards us, and the other followed Filament in the car, with one questioning eye on the officer.

Filament then came back to join the group, and seven of us stood eye to eye and said nothing.

'Let them through!' said the officer at last, suspecting he was being made to look foolish. As an afterthought, however, to appear generous and to gain face, he shouted after us, 'I've got four boys at Akure High.'

Chapter Seven

In Limbo

The setting chosen for the morning performance was a perfect Greek Amphitheatre, with three arches behind us supporting crumbling twin staircases which climbed steeply to a blue wooden door at the top. In front there were graded terraces that could seat around five hundred, and beyond, the grassy slope was shaded by a grove of trees. It was not Epidaurus, but for our purposes ideal.

We made our first entrance from the top of the stairs, for the effect was impossible to resist, and changed all our moves so that the arches became the vaulted hall of Dunsinane and the colonnades of the Rialto. We swept up and down the steps like yo-yos on a string, and kept surprising each other by appearing where least expected. It was a joyous performance, and one we will always remember for several reasons.

> Life's but a walking shadow, a poor player
> That struts and frets his hour upon the stage
> And then is heard no more; it is a tale
> Told by an idiot, full of sound and fury
> Signifying nothing.

At this point in *Macbeth*, following the death of his wife, a messenger arrives with bad news. In our resourceful adaptation I would glare off-stage, mutter 'What sayest thou?' as if more dazed than hard of hearing, repeat what he had said and then get on with it.

As I rose from my slump of bitter grief, mustering my strength for 'Liar and SLAVE!' and all that followed, a shadow fell across the stage like a cloud moving over the sun. A man quite six feet four, built like a juggernaut and as angry as he was black, lumbered up to me, grabbed a fistful of my soggy shirt and shouted, 'START AGAIN!'

'Pardon?' I quipped, for I needed time to get on top of the situation.

'My school has just arrived. We were held up by the police. You'll have to start again.'

'But we've nearly finished. A thousand children have already seen it.'

'We've come sixty miles. I've got a hundred of my best pupils with me and they're studying *Macbeth*.'

'I – could we discuss it later, do you think?' and less publicly,

I thought, though the audience were as overawed by the man's size and determination as I was, and kept a respectful silence. 'If we could just finish...' I flapped my arms helplessly.

'All right. But then, you do it again!' he threatened, and the sun came out once more as he left the stage.

I muddled through to the end of *Macbeth* and we started on *The Merchant*. While Sue filled the students in on the background of the play and the parts we would be missing out, I was crouching behind the staircase for a breathing space, mopping my brow with my cloak before leisurely donning my Shylock cap, when I felt a heavy hand on my shoulder.

'You're going to do *Macbeth* again!' the familiar voice boomed, making a statement, not asking a question.

'We're giving the whole programme again this afternoon at St Aloysius College,' I suggested. 'P'raps you could bring your pupils there...'

He shook his leonine head.

'We've got to get back before curfew. We've come sixty miles to see *Macbeth*, and my kids want to see it!'

'Well, at least they're seeing *The Merchant of Venice*,' I said. 'What an opportunity.'

'They're not *studying The Merchant of Venice*.'

I heard Sue's voice raised beyond mere projection repeating like a needle stuck in a groove, 'We are now in Venice. WE ARE NOW IN VENICE!'

Wrenching myself from the teacher's grasp and completely forgetting my Shylock gait, I leapt onto the stage like Batman –

Many a time and oft, on the Rialto you have rated me –

I directed at Sue's indignant frowns, but she didn't appreciate the joke. It's difficult to keep the ball in the air, so to speak, when half the team is off.

Shylock has never been played shiftier, for throughout the scene I kept nervously shooting glances over my shoulder expecting our imaginary Rialto to be singularly overpopulated. But the mountain of persistence contented himself with lurking behind the staircase and collaring me every time I made an exit till he wore me down.

'All right!' I capitulated. 'You realise that we have to do the whole show again this afternoon at St Aloysius College. It's going to *kill* us to do *Macbeth* again in the midday-sun, but we'll do bits or something once the ones who have already seen it have gone. Does *that* satisfy you?'

'You've made a hundred children happy,' he said, banging my shoulder like a bear.

Even allowing for the fact that our adaptations of these great classics each lasted less than an hour, there cannot be many performers who can boast of doing *The Merchant of Venice* twice and *Macbeth* three times in one day when the temperature is over ninety in the shade. For 'the bits' we were intending to do for the late arrivals spread inadvertently to the full version under the heart-warming glow of their eager appreciation.

At the end the big teacher could not be dissuaded from taking his favourite position centre-stage, where he delivered a speech and a mighty thump on both our shoulders.

'You're purple in the face,' Sue said through the wisps of steam rising from her discarded costume. 'I hope you're not going to have a heart attack.'

'I've got the symptoms,' I said. 'Isn't it supposed to start in your arm?' I rubbed the bruise that had just been inflicted.

'Good health.' Sue emptied a bottle of beer down her throat in one gulp.

'Cheers!' I said, doing likewise. 'God bless you Filament, you Hundred Watt Wonder,' I added, as our lanky Yoruba produced two more bottles, still miraculously misted from the 'fridge.

*

The Hausas were streaming out of Ibadan for their own territory in the north. Since Muritala Mohammed, a Hausa, had been assassinated, and a Yoruba, Lieutenant General Olusegun Obasanjo, was now Head of State and the Army, the whole country was afraid that intertribal differences might flare up, so the Hausas preferred to be among their own people.

The reasons for the attempted 'coup' were becoming clearer. The army of 250,000, when Nigeria has no enemies on her borders, is dangerously unwieldy. With no one to fight, officers and men in an army of that size will tend to fight among themselves, with the result that 'coups' and 'counter-coups' become endemic. Muritala Mohammed had promised to demobilise 100,000 men and hand over to civilian rule by 1979. He had also started investigation into corruption in high places. These plans were evidently unpopular among Dimka and his followers, some of whom had also been overlooked for promotion. With Dimka still free and the British refusing to extradite Gowon, frustration once more spilled over into violence.

The British Council offices had been defaced in Enugu, the heart of Ibo country, perhaps, after the Biafran war, to show Ibo loyalty to the Federal Government. The American Embassy and the British High Commission in Lagos had both been stormed and severely damaged, though the curfew continued and was strictly observed.

The port of Lagos and the airport were still closed. No one could leave or enter the country till Dimka was found, dead or alive.

*

The seasons meet in the tropical rain forest, some of the tall deciduous trees apple-green with young shoots, others copper and orange and shedding their leaves. Pale trunks festooned with creeper, palms of all varieties, the flowering flame-tree, and the silky-barked cottonwood soaring above all the others from its monumental fluted base. The high banks of foliage on either side of us converged into the middle of the road, and we were forced to slow up behind another leafy demonstration.

David sat in the front seat with Filament, cursing in Welsh. We were always in a hurry.

'It looks as if they're turning off in about a hundred yards,' he said, craning his neck through the window.

The stragglers at the rear turned to peer through our windscreen, and Sue and I tried to look as black as possible.

As the chanting crowd was filtering into a side road, Filament put his foot on the accelerator to overtake the tail end of the procession. Several of the marchers wheeled round and shouted, their faces ugly with anger. As we drew level they raised their branches above their heads and smashed them against the car.

David was struck full in the face before he had time to wind up his window. Filament swerved as a man threw himself across the bonnet with a heavy thump and pounded with the palm of his hand on the windscreen. Instinctively Filament slowed down as we were suddenly surrounded by youths, thrashing the car with the boughs they were carrying, and pressing their faces against the glass shouting unintelligible threats.

'Drive on!' David shouted. 'For God's sake, Filament, keep going!'

Filament surged forwards shedding all our attackers save the man on the bonnet, who must have hung on for almost half a mile till Filament slowed down again. Separated from the mob, he slid off much subdued, but he wrenched off a wiper in a final gesture of protest.

'Are you all right?' I asked David, who was examining the damage to his face in the driving mirror.

'No blood,' he said, though there was a hectic weal across his nose. 'I'll live. We'll have to cancel Friday's performance though,' he added. 'It would be madness to drive all the way back to Ibadan on the day of mourning. The whole country will be out, and one narrow squeak is one squeak too many as far as I'm concerned.'

'Hear, hear!' we said warmly. I was choking with frustration at the mindless injustice of generalised aggression, and I freely admit that I never wanted so much to leave Nigeria.

✳

My heart sank when David revealed that we were spending the evening with Catholic priests. Moral worth, alas, does not always guarantee that the party will go with a swing. But armed with a magnum of Chianti, we felt primed to fend off boredom.

Father Joe Davis entertained us in his quarters. He was a fat man in his fifties dressed in 'mufti' who ran a school for two thousand boys, and he was a generous and jovial host. He smoked like a chimney and drank like a fish and sprinkled his sentences with 'My God' and 'Good God' like any normal human being. In a word, he was flawless. There was also an old priest of about eighty in a white cassock who appeared to have taken a vow of silence, and a steward with two little boys to do his bidding. They had swept out our rooms and fitted up mosquito nets. Because of curfew, Sue and I were also spending the night, which was a precedent that caused a 'frisson' in Sue's and a thousand big boys' breasts, for it was the first time a woman had ever slept in this all-male establishment.

Over an excellent dinner served with chilled rosé, the conversation veered towards religion, and I felt compelled to admit to being a non-believer. Joe, as he had asked us to call him, and not 'Father' as everyone else did, was quite unperturbed, but the silent old priest shortly left without a word, and I was afraid that I had offended him. If one has spent one's life teaching and practising a faith, it is understandable after all to be upset if someone denies the reason for one's whole existence.

'Oh, don't worry about Father Michael, John,' Joe said. 'It's long past his bed-time, and anyway he doesn't really know what's going on any more, poor old chap. He hasn't spoken for seven years. It's a terrible story I'm afraid. He used to run a Mission in the north, near Kaduna, which is Hausa country. As you know, when the Ibos started the war, the Hausas and the Yorubas in retaliation tried to wipe them out. Well, Father Michael hid some Ibos in the belfry of his church, but there were informers and the Hausas found them. They dragged Michael out and forced him to watch as they threw the Ibos from the top of the tower, shooting them as they fell. He had a mental breakdown and he hasn't spoken since.'

One of the little boys passed the open door with a paint-tin on his head.

'Goodnight, Father,' he said.

'Goodnight, Sammy,' Joe waved. 'And you tell your Mummy that ju-ju won't mend her finger. Tell her to go to the hospital and they'll put it in splints.'

'Yes, Father,' Sammy said and was gone.

Seeing how Father Michael's story had saddened the company, Joe poured us all a brandy and said, 'I still marvel at how they balance everything on their head. All their possessions sometimes, in one tin-box,' he patted his balding crown, 'straight on top! You've heard about the Pidgin-English Bible, haven't you?'

We confessed that we hadn't.

'Well, some bright spark had the idea of translating the Bible into Pidgin, which would be understood practically all over Africa. I had a copy once, can't think where it's gone, but anyway the Pope banned it. There were things like...in the Lord's Prayer for example, "Forgive us our trespasses as we forgive them that trespass against us" became "We sorry for de humbug, and okay sorry for de humbug us." But the best bit was when God expelled Adam from the Garden of Eden. "Adam!" God says. "You go take your box and fuck-off!"'

We went to bed with our spirits restored.

At seven thirty the following morning he waved us goodbye, his cassock billowing in the welcome early breeze, while the whole school waited at Assembly, two thousand boys neatly dressed in blue shorts and crisply laundered shirts, standing patiently in lines for their big White Father.

※

Filament made his stage debut in our penultimate performance in Nigeria. We had waited too long for the expected numbers to turn up. As we had to finish our programme shortly after five to allow the students time to return to their school compounds before curfew, we had to do shortened versions to a pathetic handful of children.

On my first entrance as Macbeth, Sue would run to greet me, though our meeting, in deference to the African sense of decorum, was no longer a clinch but a holding of hands at arms' length. Nevertheless, when space permitted she would approach at a considerable lick, to show how pleased she was to see me and also to inject a bit of excitement. On this occasion our stage was quite big, and she came tripping towards me with her arms outstretched, but to my surprise at the very last moment she gave a little squeak and dodged past me heading straight off into 'the wings', which in this instance was a very small space indeed, containing our clothes, towels, mentholated powder, Filament with his cold-box full of Fanta and Star, a stack of broken chairs and a family of lizards. Nonplussed, I had no alternative but to follow her off to ascertain the cause of this unusual behaviour.

'What the Hell –' I spat, squeezing into the room.

'Didn't you *see* it?' Sue squealed. 'It followed me all through the letter scene, and just as you came on it touched down on my NECK!'

'What?'

'One of those horrible big black bugs!'

Nothing induced more fear or loathing in Sue than a particular insect which I suspect was a flying beetle, for it had a nasty farting kind of buzz, and it sported what appeared to be little horns and a trailing black tail. We called it the Bloody Great Bumble-Bottle.

'Oh my God! They don't bite!'

'I don't care! I can't share the stage with a Bloody Great Bumble-Bottle. *You* don't like lizards!'

'I *love* lizards! So long as they don't climb me,' I added, automatically shooting a wary glance in the direction of the stacked chairs which housed today's collection.

'Well, I love Bloody Great Bumble-Bottles, provided they're twenty miles away or dead!'

'Come on, Filament,' I said. We re-entered to clamorous applause from our small band of supporters. With their help, and considerable haloo-ing and hilarity, we cornered the bug, and a student splatted it with a dog-eared copy of the text.

We started again, but we failed to recapture the right mood for Tragedy, though *The Merchant*, considering the poor attendance, never went better.

*

Mr Jegede was a dedicated pedagogue and an ardent Maoist. With their own hands his students had built an extension to the school where we were staying, and also many of the out-buildings. They ran a chicken farm, cultivated maize and vegetables, and did all the manual work required to maintain his establishment, which in addition had an unparalleled reputation for academic achievement. With pride, he showed us a manifesto he had drawn up encapsulating his ideals: 'Students must realise that they are preparing for LIFE. They must not simply study. They must remove their trousers and get down to it!'

He guided us to a bungalow in the grounds.

'It was completed last month,' he said. 'They built it themselves in forty-two days.'

A girl in dungarees ran up and knelt at his feet.

'Mr Solaru wants to speak to you on the telephone, sir,' she said.

'Forgive me,' Mr Jegede said. 'I have been waiting for this call. Will you excuse me? I hope you will be comfortable in your little home.'

Inside, there were two bedrooms, a sitting-room, a bathroom and a kitchen. There was nothing but air in the taps which was not unusual, but neither was there even a small can of water. The entire complement of furniture was one upright chair and a broken table. There was, however, an island of hardened cement in the middle of the floor, several sacks of plaster, a carpenter's trestle and a mountain of empty paint-cans, and in one of the bedrooms there was one single bed without a mattress. Since there were four of us, Filament and David and Sue and myself, we felt the accommodation to be on the Spartan side.

'We can't stay here!' Sue said. 'We'll have to make some excuse and go back to Father Joe's.'

'You could say you've left your passport behind,' was Filament's bright suggestion, 'but we'll have to cut question-time to get there by six.'

The thought of spending the long evening imposed by the curfew in such comfortless conditions was not appealing, so we all agreed to the white lie.

Mr Jegede bounced back.

'So sorry my friends. Well, how do you like your little home? How's that for plaster-work!' he said, rubbing his hand lovingly over the smooth wall.

'Oh, the plaster-work's terrific,' I said.

'And the cupboards – look at that dove-tailing!'

'Oh, I think dove-tailing's essential...Ah...Mr Jegede...,' Sue said.

'Yes?'

'I've left my passport in Akure I'm afraid. We'll have to go back there tonight to fetch it...'

'Oh, don't worry about that. I'll telephone Father Joe and he can send one of his boys on the 'bus with it. That's no problem.'

Filament looked at Sue apologetically.

'I – well, actually, we think perhaps it would be easier for *you* if we stayed in Akure. We don't want to cause you any trouble,' David said.

'Trouble? What trouble?'

'Well, I mean, there's only one bed.'

'That's no trouble.'

'It is for three out of four of us,' David joked. 'If we leave as soon as the programme's over we can make the college by six.'

'But you can't go back to Akure – you're my guests!' He looked utterly crestfallen. 'I have it all prepared. The beds – everything is coming. I shall 'phone St Aloysius about the passport. By the time you have given your performance your little home will be ready for you.'

Sue and I looked at each other.

'It was here all the time,' she said, producing her passport from her handbag and effectively burning our boats.

'We couldn't do it to him,' she said, after our last performance in Nigeria, which had turned out to be, as looked-forward-to special occasions often are, average and unmemorable. 'It's only for one night after all, and we're leaving early for Ibadan.'

'If only he hadn't kept calling it "our little home", p'raps it wouldn't have been such a disappointment. I suppose it's quite decent, really, as far as building-sites go.'

As we arrived at the bungalow, Mr Jegede's youngest son, a mite no more than four or five years old dressed in Yoruba pyjamas, was disappearing through our front door with a carton of cornflakes twice as big as himself on his head.

We had been gone only three hours, and the transformation inside 'our little home' was so total it was difficult to grasp. The island of cement and the rest of the rubbish had vanished. There were four beds with mattresses still in their plastic envelopes, and new sheets covered in gingham counterpanes; several easy-chairs were placed around a brass coffee table, and a dining-room suite stood against the wall. There were pretty curtains on all the windows, standing lamps and fans in every room, three barrels of water in the bathroom, one of them steaming, a bowl of bougain-

villea on the table, and the 'fridge was crammed with beer and
soft drinks and bottles of Babycham.

Our dinner was brought by a file of young ladies in school uniform, who dipped to the floor with one knee in a curtsey as they
left. Rice and plantains and spinach and chicken 'soup' and beans
and bread-rolls and butter, with oranges and paw-paw and pineapple to follow. Halfway through the banquet, another procession
arrived with more of everything, and despite our protestations
the girls politely refused to take it away. On answering a shy knock
on the door, a large tray was revealed with a diminutive student
underneath. On it stood a bottle of Courvoisier, one of Avocaat
Liqueur and a box of After-Dinner mints. Finally Mr Jegede himself appeared, inquiring anxiously if there was anything we
needed.

He stayed, and we talked till after midnight about education
and politics and the future of Africa. We taught him Racing
Demon, and before we parted we toasted each other in Babycham.

For breakfast there was cornflakes and toast and marmalade and
fruit and fried eggs and boiled eggs and baked-beans and rice and
bush-meat 'soup'. If we had stayed with Mr Jegede for a week,
I could have played Falstaff without padding. He does nothing
by half-measures. He certainly removes his trousers and gets down
to it.

Chapter Eight

Trapped

'What's your favourite sign?'

We were not discussing astrology, but the painted ones above the shops and stalls that we had seen on our daily journeys.

'I like "Wee-Wee Batteries",' I said, 'though "Man Must Wack" still preoccupies me from time to time.'

'It must have been a misprint.'

'For *what*?'

' "Wack" means "Eat" in pidgin,' Filament said.

'Well that's a relief.'

'Did you see "Uncle Sammy de Tailer"?'

A strange vehicle shot past us and swung into the middle of the road. At first glance its single occupant appeared to be driving a very low, very open convertible, but further scrutiny revealed that it was in fact a saloon, and though the wheels and the rest of the working parts were clearly functioning well, the coachwork had been squashed as flat as a muffin.

'Do you think we'll ever see Cameroon?' Sue asked.

We were due in Douala the following week, but Lagos airport was still closed, and while Dimka remained free, or at least unaccounted for, there seemed little hope of being able to leave Nigeria to continue with the last lap of our tour.

'Couldn't we drive to the border and be met at the other side?' I asked David.

'You're joking! It would be far too dangerous at a time like this. Besides, it would take days, on dirt roads with no service stations – far too risky. And anyway they wouldn't let you across when you got there. The country's closed, John. You'll just have to accept that and wait.'

'Perhaps, since we seem to be trapped, we could arrange a visit to Kano and Kaduna?' Sue suggested. We had heard how beautiful the north was, with its palaces and Muslem cities of pink mud governed by emirs and sultans as flamboyant as they were rich.

'We'll work on it,' I said with enthusiasm.

'Isn't it sad to think that we've given our last performance in Nigeria.'

'Who knows? If we're stuck here for a month, p'raps we could take a few drama sessions at the university. I don't fancy just twiddling my thumbs.'

Filament drew up by the roadside where a man was standing in the shade of a tree. Hanging dead from its branches were a red patas monkey like the one that had ravished Sue, and a flying-fox. Bush-meat. They eat anything that moves. But Filament was interested in what the man was holding in his hand, a cluster of black shells, each as big as a conch, which housed the delicacy he was keen to take home as a present to his family: land snails. Before cooking, they have to be scrubbed with alum to remove the slime. He chucked them in a bucket in the boot, and by the time we arrived in Ibadan they had crept out of their shells, and their fluted suckers were sliding all over the plastic and each other. Each snail, without mincing words, resembled nothing so much as an erect human male organ (average size), surmounted by two little waving horns which instantly retract into their fat black heads if you touch them, which I didn't but Filament did. This sight failed to stimulate my digestive juices.

'I hope Filament's family are enjoying their escargots,' I said to Julia, sipping my pre-prandial drink in the luxury of the Turners' cool sitting-room. 'They must be a bit heavy on the garlic and butter.'

'If you tasted bush-meat on your travels, which I'm sure you must have, you probably ate snails though you didn't know it. Monkeys, bush-rats, daikas, snails – everything's bush-meat. It's all good protein.'

The little blond gecko that lived behind the book-case flicked out into the pool of light cast by the standard lamp, found no moths or mosquitoes, did a quick pirouette and returned to his hiding place.

'But don't worry. We're not having snails. I hope it'll be all right though. We have a new cook, and though he's very willing he has a lot to learn.'

Outside Lagos, the curfew had been lifted till eight o'clock in the evening. Bored with their own company, people had started entertaining again, though guests had to be seated soon after six.

The party included the Deputy High Commissioner and his Beautiful German Wife, and a happy, hilarious couple called Enisha. He arrived in his cassock, for he was a distinguished Methodist Preacher, whose full title was Chief the Very Reverent Doctor B.B. Enisha; his wife, who was big and white, made her entrance preceded by false eyelashes like palm-fronds, wearing a floor-length Mu-Mu with ventilation up the side that gave an uninterrupted view of an improbable expanse of knicker.

'I couldn't get the old bugger to change!' were the first words she spoke.

Throughout the evening her conversation was scattered with a defiant number of four-letter words. 'B.B.', as she called her husband, chortled indulgently at her intemperate language, and reproved her only once, and that was not for swearing but for biting his ear.

When I expressed surprise and amusement at 'B.B.'s' tolerance, considering his calling, she said, 'Listen, darling. He's my third, and I warned him before I married him that he'd have to accept me as I am. I was an actress, you see – we must have lots of friends in common,' and we did. 'My first husband was a pouf, my second kicked the bucket, so third time lucky is what I say.' And that was when she bit him. Very gently.

The new cook showed promise, though getting at the beef-olives through the coils of knotted string proved tricky, and while the fish was served 'au naturel', the ice-cream, due to a misunderstanding, had melted away under a topping of hot parsley sauce.

'If twenty-five policemen with rifles don't make you nervous, come to dinner tomorrow night,' the Deputy High Commissioner's Beautiful German Wife said.

'How do you fit them all round the table?'

She thought I was serious.

'They stay in the garden, night and day.'

'That's very kind. We'd love to.'

'Jonathan's getting so bored being at home all day, poor darling. He loves visitors. We daren't send him to school at the moment in case he's kidnapped. Things might get better after tomorrow...' The day of public mourning. More demonstrations were expected, and the British were being advised to keep a low profile. 'If you're still here at the end of the week, we could go riding at the Polo Club on Saturday.'

'Smashing!'

'Good. I'll have to borrow a car though. For once, C.D. plates are a disadvantage.'

We told them the story of the night of the ants, and, as is usual with much-travelled people, they topped it.

'We had to stop once at a rarely used Rest-House in Persia, and there were cockroaches in the loo the size of lobsters. The children had to have some sleep, so we stuffed newspapers round the door, put their sleeping-bags on the billiard-table, and sat up all night keeping watch.'

'That's nothing. We were invited to eat with a Sheik in Saudi Arabia. As we went into the dining room we could see a bowl the size of a tractor-wheel in the middle of the table, overflowing with glistening caviare – well you know how rich those sheiks can be. As we approached it though, I'm sorry to say, all the "caviare" rose in a cloud with a hideous buzz, and underneath there was nothing but fly-blown yoghurt.'

At that Mrs Enisha said, 'Shit!', so we resumed more civilised conversation.

✱

The day of mourning passed without violence. Sir Martin Le Quesne was pilloried in the press, however, for putting in a claim to the Military Government for the damage done to the High

Commission building when it had been attacked. He was perfectly within his rights, but in the prevailing political climate it was considered to be an undiplomatic move. The resentment finally grew to such proportions that he was called back to England, and his post in Lagos was re-filled.

*

The woman looked too old to be pregnant. Her legs were thin as sticks and the skin on her neck hung in folds like a tortoise's. Her hair stuck out in unkempt bunches and was grey with dust and specks of lint. She ran through the crowded market using her distended belly as a battering-ram, scattering vegetables and fruit amid a storm of protest. Two men in ragged shorts ran after her, one wielding a stick, and the other a long slender whip which he carried upright like a wireless aerial. The first man to overtake her smashed her across the shoulders with his stick, and the hag's knees buckled beneath her. In silence she crouched with her hands guarding her unborn child, as the second man joined the first, laying into her with no quarter.

'Dear God,' I said to Filament, who had brought us to the market to buy last-minute presents. 'Can't we do something?'

Filament grimly shook his head.

But suddenly the woman twisted round and caught the stick as it landed on her back. She yanked it from the man's hand and rose to her feet with a shriek to freeze the blood. A monkey that was tethered to a stall nearby appeared to beckon to the crowd like a fairground tout, chattering with glee and clapping his hands, and pointing with excitement at the scene in progress.

Swinging the stick about her head, the woman loosed a volley of abuse at her attackers, and though the man carrying the whip landed another couple of blows across her breasts his fury visibly abated in the face of her tirade. Though she was old and pregnant and no match for their combined strength, they both began to cower under her torrent of vituperation, till first they slunk off sheepishly, then finally ran away. Even after they had disappeared from sight, she continued to rail for the benefit of the crowd that had collected. Still muttering, she flung the stick down in disgust, and, exactly like a dog that has won a scrap, she went behind a

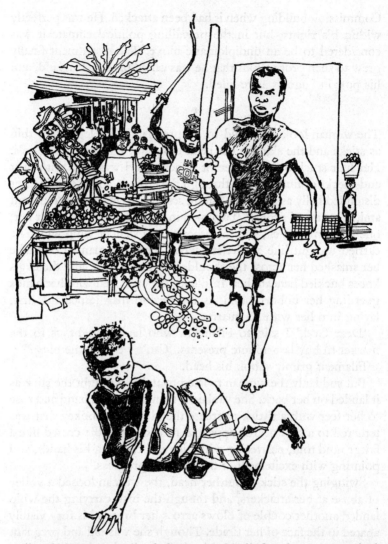

stall and, fixing us with a defiant stare, hitched up her wrapper and squatted urinating on the ground.

'I've never seen such a reversal! I was sure they were going to kill her,' Sue said.

'What did she say, Filament? I've never witnessed a finer example of the power of the spoken word.'

'Well, you know what they say about women's tongues...'

'What was it all about?'

'I don't know for sure,' Filament said. 'She might just have been a thief, or an unfaithful wife, of course, but she was cursing like a ju-ju Mammy and invoking bad magic, so I think she must have been a witch.'

'She certainly scared me,' I said.

'Which isn't difficult!' Sue and I recited in unison.

'Do you believe in witchcraft?'

'I'm a Christian, John,' he said, which wasn't an answer. 'But for those who believe in it, it works. When they first put up the telephone system in Ibadan, thieves kept stealing the wire, because it was made of copper, which fetches a high price. They got a witch-doctor to put ju-ju on the poles, and it hasn't happened since.'

'Blimey.'

'Only a year ago in Onitsha – that's a fairly sophisticated part of the country, in the Eastern State – a sixteen-year-old boy was accused of putting the evil-eye on a man, and dwindling him.'

' "Dwindling"? You mean –' I waggled my little finger suggestively.

'Yes. Making him impotent. Enough people believed that the boy was responsible, so they tore him apart.'

'Good God.'

'This is the place for Ayo-boards,' he said, leading the way into an alley where a phalanx of stall-holders converged on us to pluck us by the sleeve. Filament was brusque and protective, and once we had chosen what we wanted he haggled indefatigably on our behalf.

This ancient game, which is reputed to be as old as man, is played throughout Africa under different names, sometimes, as in antiquity, with pebbles placed in hollows scooped out of the desert sand.

Whenever I play it, I am aware of an almost spooky feeling of the timelessness of Africa and all mankind.

But perhaps that pregnant witch cast a spell on me.

*

We spent almost a week playing tennis and swimming and going out to dinner with friends and our spongebags. We went riding with the D.H.C.'S B.G.W., an outing spoiled only by a plague of silent fluffy flies, that stuck to our faces and our clothing in a dully-glinting, pewter-grey rash. The curfew was finally lifted completely, except in Lagos, but still the airport and the frontiers remained closed, and though we at first enjoyed the rest we quickly tired of our life as permanent guests. We were advised to abandon our plan to visit the north and any hope of teaching at the university while the anti-British feeling persisted. We had reluctantly decided that we would have to go straight back to England as soon as we were allowed to leave, when Gordon burst in with the news that all flights had resumed.

'One more day and we'd have had to cancel Cameroon,' I said, and Sue and I hugged each other with relief.

'Do you want me to try to get you onto the first flight to Douala?' Gordon asked tentatively.

The cheerless vision of Lagos and its airport, congested at the best of times, rose before us.

'Do you have any influence?' I asked, hardly daring to hope.

'No, in a word,' Gordon said. 'I think you'll just have to go there and wait.'

'That's what I was afraid you'd say.'

Unless one could secure a room at the dreaded Airport Hotel, and after the long isolation of the country this would be out of the question, it would be impossible to do in Lagos what one might do in times of crisis in other cities, that is, visit the airport daily till a flight-booking is confirmed, for there is not enough time in the day, or patience in human nature, to sit daily in a traffic-jam for five hours, fight through the mob at the airport to find anyone with any information or authority to supply one with a valid ticket, then, if one is disappointed, spend another five gruelling hours crawling back from whence one came. We would have to sleep on the pavement.

'I'm not going on the first flight,' Sue said, though she didn't actually stamp her foot. 'We've been through Lagos Airport with normal traffic, and after being closed for weeks – no way!'

It was not, perhaps a constructive statement, but it was positive.
'I'll try for the second day,' said Gordon, looking a bit grey
under the eyes.

'Lagos, here we come,' I groaned.

'Let's not even think about it yet,' Sue said.

The headline in the morning paper said, '22,000 SLEEP OUT AT
AIRPORT.'

*

I prefer to swelter in silence, but Sue likes to keep cool even if the
air-conditioning sounds like a pneumatic-drill. One can get used
to either the discomfort or the noise, provided there is continuity,
but to be plunged at ten-minute intervals all through the night
from a peaceful oven into a rackety refrigerator is a classic antidote to sleep.

After yet more presents and goodbyes, we had left Ibadan at
dawn. The drive took much longer than it would have done at
normal times, with road-blocks and long delays, while the army
with rifles and the police with whips still sought Mohammed's
elusive murderer. Our hosts in Lagos had taken us to their Re-
creation Club for dinner at High-Tea-Time, as we had to be locked
in by eight, and they apologised that the curfew prevented them
from taking us to the naughtiest nightclub in Africa. We were
indeed disappointed, as some naughtiness might have dispelled
a little of the gloom that this appalling city cast on us.

'Are you asleep?' Sue whispered, switching off the air-conditioner for the twentieth time.

'That's a joke in bad taste,' I snarled through gritted teeth. 'On,
off, on, off, all bloody night. Can't you leave it one way or the
other?'

'I've been poisoned,' she said.

I sat bolt upright.

'What?'

'I've got the runs.'

'You've got gippy tummy, you mean. You haven't been poisoned. Poisoned! You do exaggerate.'

'I've got the runs, and I've been throwing up, and I feel quite
dreadful,' she said, pitifully clutching her stomach.

'Oh my God.' I was contrite. 'I'm sorry. Is it malaria again, do you think?'

She shook her head. 'I don't think so. It's just Lagos tummy as you say, but needing the loo as I do every five minutes, how am I going to get through that five-hour traffic jam?'

It was a good question. We filled her up with Lomatol and Kaolin and prayed. Sue exercised heroic self-control, and we made it to the airport with only three stops at establishments along the way, which, though unsalubrious, nevertheless had plumbing.

The congestion was not as bad as we had feared, though outside a great crowd was surging, held at bay by troops of soldiers wielding sticks, with rifles slung across their backs. Filament stayed with us, in case our efforts to leave on the Cameroon flight should prove unsuccessful.

They could not guarantee us places. The time for boarding came and went, but still we waited with no information. Sue huddled miserably in a corner, while I discussed with Filament the pros and cons of spending the night in the car or on the pavement.

A party of Japanese businessmen sat opposite us in shirt-sleeves, acting inscrutable. The wife of one was feeding her three dolls of children with black cabbage stuffed with rice. The youngest was in a push-chair and was suffering from measles, or what looked like it, for she was covered in red spots. A baby Nigerian girl of the same age, her hair a spikey halo of short plaits, with gold rings twinkling in each tiny ear-lobe, wandered close to watch. The two babies, one yellow and spotty, the other black and spiky, stared unblinking at each other with mutual satisfaction for quite half an hour.

Filament was preparing the car for sleeping in when it was announced that our 'plane was departing. We were dubious about joining the scrum again, since we had been called five hours earlier on a false alarm, but this time passengers were going through. Our only regret at leaving then was in parting with our remarkable Yoruba driver. In the words of an accolade I once received from a New York taxi-driver for overtipping because I had no change, if ever there was one, Filament was 'a gentleman, a scholar, and a top-banana'.

Chapter Nine

Cameroon

The Union Jack fluttering on the bonnet of our chauffeur-driven limousine was a symbol to us of the difference in the political climate between Nigeria and Cameroon. One step across the border and we were in a different world. It was like 'being abroad' in the English sense, for Douala is French-speaking, and the architecture, the broad boulevards lined with palm-trees, the advertisements for 'Dubonnet' and 'Disque Bleu', and the pervasive aroma of garlic and black tobacco, were all more reminiscent of Europe than of Africa. The British Consul, Julian Lamble, had whisked us through the formalities at the neat little airport, and out through the sweet-smelling streets to our comfortable hotel in the town, La Falaise, which overlooked the harbour, where gleaming liners en route for the south and the Ivory Coast lay at anchor, suspended, now that night was falling, in the pale amber of flood-lighting.

As we registered at the desk, the svelte receptionist, wearing a Hermès silk blouse, slipped the menu for the evening meal into its display-case. There was pâté de foie, moules marinières, veau cordon bleu, champignons and petits pois and mousse au chocolat and lots more besides, and the wine-list was a slim volume. In the bedroom, there was a little packet in the wardrobe which said 'Prophyltex Gratuit'.

Over a pernod and salted almonds, Julian explained that our programme had simply been postponed for a week, so that we would have Saturday and Sunday to ourselves.

The terrace of the Akwa Palace is not the Champs Elysées, but the passing scene is more exotic. We were pestered by traders cajoling us to buy bags of snakeskin and ostrich-skin and clandestine bundles of contraband diamonds, which could be bits of glass; bangles of ivory and elephant hair set in gold and silver, seven-day rings, with a ring for each day of the week linked with little golden tassles; tiger's teeth mounted in filigree; batiks and embroidered shirts; old masks and ostrich eggs and rearing horsemen worked in brass; collages made from the wings of fabulous butterflies, mutilated and chopped up to make luminous pictures of flowers and birds, and verdant decomposing landscapes.

'Ça c'est horr*eeeb*le!' Sue said, in an accent that made Edward Heath's sound like General de Gaulle. 'Allez-vous en!' and she pushed the man away in disgust.

'You do your first performance on Monday at Buea, that's at the foot of Mount Cameroon. It's a pretty spot, so I've arranged for you to go up on Sunday, if you'd like to – there's an annual race up the mountain, and you might find it amusing. It's sponsored by Guinness, so it's a bit of a free-for-all. There's no actual climbing involved, just a sprint up ten thousand feet to the lip of the volcano, then down again. The record so far is five hours up and down. Are you interested?'

'Five hours? Ten thousand feet? Well, ah – as a matter of fact, Julian, ah – hill-climbing is not actually my speciality. It's nice of you to ask.'

'Not to compete, you fool! Most of them train all the year round. Just as a spectator.'

'Oh, great!'

'In the meantime, if you're desperate for something to do tomorrow night, you can come to the DADS.'

'Pardon?'

'The Douala Amateur Dramatic Society.'

'What are they doing?' Sue asked, shooting me one of her cautionary looks.

'H.M.S. Pinafore.'

'We won't be *that* desperate,' I laughed.

'I'm in it,' Julian said.

'OH! Well, we'd love to come! Wouldn't we, Sue?'

'Yes,' she said, though she shamelessly covered her eyes with her hand and shook her head.

*

'It's not fair. All that haute cuisine and chilled white Burgundy, and all I could face was an egg.'

'Think how much more you're going to enjoy it when you're better.' I inanely sought for words of comfort. 'And it'll give us a good excuse to leave if it's dreadful.'

'Do you want to put something on it?'

We joined the throng that was shuffling up the steps of the hall.

'I once did bits from *the Mikado* at a school concert,' I admitted. 'I wore my sister's galoshes and a cardboard hat, and my mother died the following week.'

'It'll be good for the diary,' Sue said, which was a palliative we were both wont to use for extreme suffering.

I have seen *H.M.S. Pinafore* only once, as rendered by the DADS of Douala, and for reasons only marginally connected with the talents of Messrs. Gilbert and Sullivan it was an evening of undiluted joy.

I shall always see the quarter-deck of this quintessentially English vessel thinly populated with men of disparate size and shade attempting to dance the hornpipe, looking as much like sailors as the Dagenham Girl Pipers do the Black Watch Band. Able-Seaman Deadeye had the shape of an avocado but the colour of an aubergine, and though his voice was treacly-rich he sang with the accents of Maurice Chevalier. The women were undisguiseably secretarial, with the odd Council wife thrown in, except for Buttercup the Bumboat Woman, for whom the epithet 'rosy' was not apt in this production, though she did wear an orange wig and an inordinate amount of rouge which showed up in strong lighting. The Captain's Daughter looked like his mother, though she had a pretty voice when one could hear it. We referred to her as 'the Toucan', for her face was predominantly composed of nose, with just enough room on either side for eyes. Noses tend to be inexpressive, and, in Dorothy Parker's immortal phrase, the Toucan's face went through 'the whole gamut of emotions, from

A to B'. She was the incarnation of 'Nanny' in the story of the
tactless little boy and his tactful sister. 'Oh, Nanny!' says the
little boy, 'What an ENORMOUS nose!' 'Don't worry, Nanny,' says
his little sister, 'You've got the TINIEST little eyes!'

Julian played the First Lord of the Admiralty with a small false
moustache. Knowing a little of the problems from the other side
of the footlights, I guessed that he was having difficulty with
this artificial flourish on his upper lip when he started to finger it
constantly as though he had the toothache. I could see it flap on
all the explosive consonants, particularly 'p', and I suspected it
would be only minutes before he and his hirsute appendage would
part company for good. The atmosphere was stifling, the uniforms
looked genuinely designed for the British climate, so it is no
reflection on the adhesive properties of Max Factor's Spirit Gum
that it was insufficient to avert catastrophe on a sweltering
evening in Equatorial Africa.

Singing requires more precise techniques than straight acting.
Principal among the differences between the two, perhaps, is the
need for a singer not only to hold a larger quantity of air in his
lungs, but also, since the musical line cannot be held up, and
in a work like this the complexity of W. S. Gilbert's lyrics requires
very precise articulation, it is imperative that he refill his lungs
quickly.

> Never mind the why and wherefore,
> Love can level ranks, and therefore
> Though your nautical relation
> In my set could surely *P*ass,
> Though you occu*P*y a station
> In the lower middle class...

Two 'p's did it. For a split second Julian's moustache floated
free of his drenched upper lip, then he snatched a deep breath
and swallowed it.

He was not alone in having tears in his eyes.

*

Far from being 'a sprint up a mountain', the Annual Race up
Mount Cameroon is one of the toughest challenges to human
endurance. It starts in the sub-tropical little town of Buea, which

nestles among tea-plantations like four-foot deep green carpets, at a height of three thousand feet, and continues for thirty kilometres up through the seasons to ten thousand feet, where the lunar landscape round the crater is composed of crusted lava and volcanic dust, often covered in snow, and always swept with biting, sub-zero winds. The volcano is active, and due to erupt, but in the past there has always been enough warning to evacuate the town, and casualties have so far been avoided. About two hundred competitors take part, including farmers, students, accountants, mountain-guides, shepherds, and this year a Swiss-Presbyterian priest from a mission in Garoua. There are no rules. If you could get up and down on a bicycle, there would be nothing to stop you from trying. All entrants must have a doctor's certificate and a security bracelet of identity which is locked, and the army monitor the whole show as an exercise, with walkie-talkies at strategic points all the way to the top.

The feeling in the crowd was high. Though the prize of £200 (Guinness also donates a further £200 to charity) may not seem princely, apart from the prestige, to a poor shepherd in Cameroon £200 is a lot of money. There is keen competition between villages, for should one of their own runners win, they expect a share of the bounty.

A brass band in red tunics and an orchestra of tribal drums vied for attention. There were little stalls everywhere proclaiming 'Guinness is good for you!' and 'Buvez Guinness! C'est toujours bon!' And at eight o'clock in the morning, already there was a wobble of a few jolly drunks.

One hundred and seventeen young aspirants came jogging through the town in Guinness tee-shirts and little white caps, cheered on by a jubilant crowd of several thousands. One European, who was no longer a stripling, carried not one but two walking-sticks, to the boundless amusement of the onlookers.

Once they were almost out of sight over the first rise, strung out already over half a mile, since it was raining intermittently and there was nothing to do but drink Guinness and get wet, we adjourned to our hotel to wait, calculating precisely, as the unbroken record to date had been five hours, when to return to be in plenty of time to hail the winner.

When we arrived back, however, it was to a scene of great consternation. Several runners who had given up or collapsed were lying about being fanned with towels or slaked with cold drinks and even Guinness. But what had thrown the crowd of ten thousand into a babble of disbelief was that the winner had already returned, only three hours and fifty minutes after starting, knocking one hour and ten minutes off the existing record. The army could only confirm that he had reached the summit, and there could be little room for a mistake, since he was the only white man in the race. For Walter Stifter, the Tyrolean missionary, though also an athlete with an Olympic-Team trial behind him, had achieved at thirty-two years of age this near-impossible feat, by using his two walking sticks which had been scoffed at, in the descent, like a skier, swinging between them all the way to the bottom. There was less feeling of jubilation than of outrage, that the winner was not only a European but a cheat. Perhaps next year they will draw up regulations.

❋

Though some of the students were francophone, and few were studying the plays, the performance in Buea in a hall built of volcanic rock, with the mist-swathed mountain visible through the open eaves, was politely and well received, and it was a pleasure for us to be working again, and in an atmosphere free from tension.

We dined with six Catholic fathers, one Cameroonian, one Irishman, one Glaswegian, one Dutchman and two from Mill Hill. Yet again we found priests to be sparkling company and lavish hosts.

'It's enough to convert one to Catholicism,' I said to Sue, as we returned replete to our bungalow-hotel. 'With all that scrumptious food and wine, no wonder they have inner peace.'

But flippancy aside, the missionaries we met were enough to shake the faith of the most devout atheist.

❋

Our British Council escort in Cameroon was a sauncey unmarried woman called Shirley, who augmented her night's sleep by snatching little naps throughout our performance – which was not encouraging. In truth, she had but recently recovered from a serious operation, and the journeys by Land Rover over unmade roads were debilitating, though she never complained. She was killing two birds with one stone on our tour, by delivering boxes of books for the school libraries – part of the Aid Programme – and at Kumba 'The Handing Over of the Books' became a ceremony of some weight.

We arrived late and flustered, having spent an hour and a half in the only bank in the area cashing traveller's cheques. Beaming clerks had pottered about with forms in quadruplicate, shuffling carbons like Tommy Cooper muffing a trick, repeating, 'Oh, you are welcome', then passing more forms on to the others to have fun with, chuckling with delight at their esoteric skill in thus spinning out such a simple transaction. They had been amazed and quite perturbed when we had expressed impatience, and only a full explanation of our purpose in Cameroon, delivered to a 'tutting' and 'clicking' glee-club that formed on the other side of the counter to hear our unlikely story, had persuaded them to hand over the money at all.

After a bone-shaking drive through virgin forest, the silver barks smothered in draped curtains of creeper, past slow, swollen rivers fringed with palms, their blue-black surfaces dotted with islands and floating with acid-green sedge, we crawled at last into Kumba behind a herd of humped cattle, honking our horn but succeeding only in scattering the indignant colony of white egrets that fed off their ticks.

At the school, all the teachers were gathered together, though the principal guest had evidently been notified of our failure to appear. As befitted a man of his eminence, he was waiting for our arrival before making his entrance.

Cameroon is Gerald Durrell country, and to anyone who has read *The Bafut Beagles* the title of NFON will be familiar. It simply means 'Chief', though there are lesser chiefs called WHUMS and other resounding names. (WHUM III, we saw in a newspaper, whom we thought might be described as 'next door to the bathWHUM'.) But our NFON, however, the NFON of Kumba, who was anxiously awaited to be the Official Receiver of the Books, was a different NFON, and a gentleman of awesome importance. He is a Paramount Chief, and the son of a Paramount Chief. His father had sixty wives, and after his death the funeral cortège that followed his body included three hundred of his children.

A silence fell on the company as the group crossed the school compound, with His Highness the NFON of Kumba leading by several paces. He was a slender, studious-looking man in an embroidered gown wearing a red pill-box hat. As he approached the assembled staff, Shirley, Sue and myself were suddenly quite literally exposed as everyone else dropped to their knees. The headmaster shuffled to his feet and introduced us, though a handshake and an inclination of the head seemed almost discourteous surrounded by all this obeisance. His highness, however, was most civil, and he led the way inside the school building graciously brushing aside the apologies for our late arrival.

The large parcel of books was on a table in a narrow passage. It was not the roomiest situation for a meeting of this solemnity, but the NFON took up a resolute stance, so the rest of us deferentially splayed out in a wide arc along the corridor.

Speeches were made thanking 'Her Britannic Majesty's Government' for 'this timely gift', scattered with ringing phrases like 'the Thirst for Knowledge', and 'the Quest for Truth'. Shirley acquitted herself well as the queen's representative, and the parcel was opened. The formal structure of the meeting collapsed, as teachers and some senior pupils who had gathered to watch tumbled about the contents like children round the tree on Christmas morning. Their genuine excitement showed, if any proof were needed, how desperately short of books are the developing countries.

At the reception afterwards, the NFON said to me, 'You are with the British Council too?'

'No, sir. I'm an actor. We're doing *Macbeth* and *The Merchant of Venice* for schools.'

'Ah, of course. I've heard about this. Do you appear in films too?'

'Yes. I've made quite a few films.'

'I am very fond of the cinema. I don't have much opportunity now, but when I was in Eltham, just after the Second World War, I used to go to the Essoldo every Saturday. Perhaps I have seen you in something?'

'Well – 1945 – I rather think...'

'Now wait! Yes! Your face is familiar...Of course! I remember you! You were one of "The Three Stooges"!'

*

Sue lifted the Haig's whisky bottle to her lips and swallowed half the contents in one gulp. Mine had Cinzano on the label, and we scarcely noticed any longer the parozone fumes from the water-purifying tablets. It was ice-cold from the 'fridge, and its wetness was a wonder of the world.

'That was the hottest yet,' Sue gasped, sprinkling herself from the bottle like a bag-full of chips.

'You say that every time.'

'No, but it's true. I thought I was going to faint. Didn't you see me sway in the Casket scene?'

'I thought that was emotion.' I was struggling vainly with my boots, but suction and swollen feet had effected a permanent bond. 'No good asking you,' I muttered, assuming Sue would understand what I was talking about by the telepathy that grows between people who spend so much time together. She was spread-eagled on a heap of sacks, gurgling at her bottle, careless of her costume which had to last out for only three more performances. 'I'll have to waken Shirley.'

But our chauffeur came to the rescue, as we had a long drive before nightfall and he was anxious to be under way.

In Buea, we had been so close to the mountain that we had been deceived into thinking that the first ridge was the summit, but as we sped south we saw Mount Cameroon in its entirety, a pale, gigantic silhouette with a low girdle of cloud, filling the horizon. A watery white sun was setting over the forest, and in the deepening gloom the bright colours seemed neon-lit in contrast, fat fists of green bananas swaying on top of heads, a scarlet umbrella like a ball of fire flickering between the trees. The smell of the rubber plantations, so different from that of the processed stuff, musky and organic and refreshing. Files of baby girls, some little more than toddlers with pots and pails and basins spilling over on their heads, risked disaster by removing one steadying-hand to wave to us. Men and women passed dripping from the river clad in wrappers. Villages that in the heat of day seemed deserted burgeoned in the cool of evening. Groups lounged chatting on their slatted verandahs, babies suckling, women being combed and plaited and coiffeured, one treadling an ancient sewing-machine. Making fires, sweeping, pounding, cooking. Bands of carefree convicts in coarse striped cotton, singing while they wielded their shovels by the roadside. They were happy to be alive in a country where robbery is a capital offence.

'I wonder if they've caught Dimka yet?'

'Doesn't Nigeria seem a long way off?' Sue said.

Though most people thought that he must have slipped out of the country, they found him in the end, and he was taken onto Ba-Ba beach outside Lagos with his fellow-conspirators, and shot. Sue, with her customary bad taste, referred to it thereafter as 'Bye-Bye Beach'.

＊

We walked onto the stage in the Baptist School dining-room, and the girls burst into peals of laughter. I instinctively glanced down, fearing that perhaps my jock-strap was not fulfilling its function after two months on the road, but it was still holding out, or maybe, more accurately, holding in.

'What's so funny? This is a bit of a blow for our pre-penultimate,' I whispered to Sue as the laughter continued.

'You put your arm round my waist when you helped me up,' Sue said.

'Oh come on! It can't be just that.'

Then the girls screamed and pointed. On the window sill behind us, a family of baboons was sitting like paying customers. The adults craned their necks, alternately raising and lowering their beetle brows in amazement, while a baby, who was picking nonchalantly at his mother's pelt, suddenly lifted her tail to gaze intently at her anal aperture as though awaiting a revelation.

'Competition!' I said. Then, 'They've heard about your rapport with monkeys.'

A member of the staff successfully drove them off, barking crossly.

As the uproar subsided, we were preparing to start when a

senior prefect stepped up onto the stage to make a shy speech of welcome. She then turned with a sharp command, and the audience rose to its feet. She raised her voice in a long clear note, and the whole school joined her in glorious harmony. They sang racy rhythmic hymns for us, 'A river of peace, an ocean of love', swaying to the music and clapping their hands. We would have been content to listen to them all morning.

Thus 'warmed-up', the performance went with a swing. We had a lively question session, and more than the usual number of requests for our addresses.

'If everyone who says they're going to write to us does it,' Sue said, 'we'll need a typing pool.'

We did receive many letters, but one reply to each has so far seemed sufficient to establish that we are 'pen-friends', without a heavy correspondence ensuing. Since I loathe writing letters, I am grateful for their lack of tenacity.

The compound was built around perfectly manicured lawns studded with flower-beds on an undulating slope overlooking the sea. Breakers pounded on the black rocks, where dug-out canoes were beached under the haphazard palms, while across the bay was strung a necklace of little islands smothered in foliage. Behind us, Mount Cameroon was a monumental backcloth.

While we sipped a beer on the principal's terrace, kite-hawks drifted overhead searching for a movement in the lush undergrowth.

'The Church Youth Club has just started a Drama Section,' the principal told us. 'One of the members asked me if you'd care to stay on after your programme this afternoon and watch some excerpts they've prepared from *Hamlet*. I've no idea what it'll be like.'

We managed to switch on tactful smiles.

'Of course.' What else could we say?

*

Our penultimate performance was merely an hors d'œuvre to the entrée of the Drama Club's offering. We could sense that the audience was restless, being composed largely of adults who had

167

not studied the plays, so we did shortened versions and ended to tepid applause. After changing, we joined Shirley in 'the stalls' to await we knew not what.

It was often extremely difficult for Sue and myself to understand Africans when they spoke English, as we were never in one place long enough to get used to their varying accents. But knowing *Hamlet* fairly well, I expected to be able to follow the scenes with ease.

A young man came on to introduce the programme. I gathered that he would play Claudius. He apologised that, due to casting problems, the actor in the eponymous role was unfortunately too young, being under seventy-five, which he assured us was the right age to play *Hamlet*. He told us a little about the play, my only reservation about his telling of the plot being that, although there is ample evidence to suggest that Hamlet was extremely fond of his mother, I would take issue with the young man's contention that he actually, if I understood him correctly, humped' her. Indeed, if Hamlet is supposed to be seventy-five, a simple sum leads one to the inescapable conclusion that 'humping' his mother is not only an unattractive idea, it could hasten her end. Since Gertrude was not appearing, however, we would be spared any illustration of his thesis.

Hamlet, when he came on, was indeed fifty years too young for the part, and he appeared to be drunk. He wore a gown just short enough to reveal the splendour of his purple platform-soled boots, and I understood, 'Oh, my offence is rank!' and nothing more. To say that we were puzzled is an understatement. I have worked with groups of black actors in the townships in South Africa, who, without any opportunities to gain experience and without ever having seen professionals in a live show, have an instinctive talent for the theatre which is unique. I can only suppose that this 'Drama Group' of two had been convened on the spur of the moment by two simple-minded young men with exhibitionistic tendencies, perhaps to play an elaborate joke which misfired, or possibly in the vain hope that an audience would transform their undigested ideas into a 'happening'.

The onlookers, as embarrassed as we, began to leave one by one, till there was no one left but Sue and me and Shirley (fast asleep).

They were still at it when we slipped away without a word of congratulation or encouragement – hardly a triumph for British Diplomacy – but there was nothing constructive to say.

✻

'Why can't I just kick it in?' I asked petulantly.

'Please restrain yourself, sir,' said the under-manager of the hotel, placing himself between me and my bedroom door, the lock of which had immovably jammed. 'Don't worry. We will find a carpenter for you in the morning.'

'But I *am* worried! All my things – clean drawers, prickly-heat powder, tooth-brush – everything! They're all *in* there!' I said, making another futile effort to turn the key. 'And we're leaving tomorrow morning at some ungodly hour to catch a 'plane. I've got to pack.'

'At seven o'clock, to be precise,' Shirley added, homing in on the disturbance.

'I'm very sorry, sir, but there's nothing we can do until the morning. We'll have a carpenter here at six.'

'But –'

'You can sleep in my room,' Sue said.

'That's sweet of you,' I said. The under-manager meaningfully purloined the key. 'And don't try charging me my room rate for tonight,' I threw at his departing, uncooperative back, though he could hardly be blamed for what the humidity, no doubt, had caused. Under-managers, however, must be prepared to suffer a little unreasonable abuse. 'I'll go down and order dinner...'

'Our second-last night in the Dark Continent,' Sue said later, examining the shooting stars made by the refracting harbour lights in her wine-glass. 'Two months is just about right, don't you think? I'm sad to be leaving and happy to be going home in about equal proportions.'

'Julie Andrews left me her *Evening Standard*,' I said, referring to an English air-hostess we had met earlier in the lobby. 'What's going on at home all seems so remote and unimportant. But then, perhaps reading about Africa when we get back to London will feel the same.'

She shook her head. 'Not if we read about the countries we've visited. They're not just areas on a map any more.'

'Travelling as a tourist is so dull, by comparison.'

'It's the people I'll remember, even more than the places.'

'And the bugs. Here's to the people, and down with the bugs.'

'I'll drink to that.'

The waves were lapping at the terrace below our feet, and voices floated across the water keening 'soul' to a leisurely, late-night pulsing of the drums.

'Let's go to bed.'

The music was still playing at six o'clock in the morning when the carpenter arrived to fix my lock. This revelry was not unusual, we were told, for a wedding-party.

Chapter Ten

Closing Night

On our last day in Yaounde the Mango rains let up, and the sun ripped through the banks of grey clouds, slicing through the humidity, and honing the tiles by the free-form pool to the temperature of hot-plates impossible for bare feet to patter across. The tarmac bubbled, the grass steamed, and Sue and I sprawled on it like mad dogs surrendering to the rapacious rays for the last time before returning to an English winter. We plunged from time to time into the glittering turquoise water which caressed my hectic flush like wild silk, and multi-coloured birds whistled in a lilac jacaranda that trailed a sky-shadow of its fallen petals over the misty lawn.

We ate salad niçoise with rosé in a circular tower under a concrete mushroom the size of a minor planet, and gazed out over the wooded hills of Cameroon.

'Not suffering too much?'

Sue shook her head.

'Happy,' was all she said.

❈

The students piled into the lecture-room at the University of Yaounde filling every available space. Fire-regulations were brazenly flouted. They sat on the stairs, they squatted on the floor, they crowded into the exits spilling out the open doors into the darkened corridor beyond. The hum of the air-conditioning was distracting, and Sue and I had our usual difference of opinion.

171

'With all those bodies, and the lights, we'll melt!' she complained.

'Let's have it off for the first half, and if it gets too hot we'll put it on for the second.'

And I won, and we kept it off, and you could hear a pin drop.

Last nights are always emotional, even if the experience has not been wholly enjoyable, but ours had been special in every way, and it was like saying goodbye forever to someone you love. As each favourite moment arrived, we saw it as freshly as the first time, because it was also the last. There is a heightened consciousness of time passing, and an unbearable nostalgia that gives to a final performance a different feeling from the excitement of a first night, but it raises it above the humdrum, and, with an audience as responsive as the University Students of Yaounde, the evening became a fitting end to our tour. There was no question-time, as we were returning in the morning for a proper seminar, but many well-wishers stayed behind for an informal talk, or just to shake us warmly by the hand.

'The Savoy was never like this,' Sue said, after we had indulged in a little physical contact.

'They've spoiled us for English audiences, I'm afraid,' I said. 'I feel like getting sloshed.'

*

The walls of the 'cave' trembled and the ground shook with the pounding of the music from the disco-speakers. The tiny dance-floor under the dim red lights was writhing with couples like the Lowest Circle of Hell. The reception that had been given in our honour was a friendly though sedate affair, enlivened for an un-planned moment by the unexpected appearance of Shirley's wicked little wild dog from Tunis who escaped from his place of confinement and skidded among the guests, leaping the furniture, savagely growling and wagging his curly tail simultaneously, and swiping a chipolata on a stick from the very hand of the British Ambassador. As the distinguished guests began to leave, we had been whisked off by a Real Cool Cameroon Party to the sexiest nightclub outside the Reperbahn, where we were now imprisoned in noise, as the deaf are in silence.

I returned to the table with a round of drinks, just as the squelch and thunder of the reggae stopped for a blessed moment.

'We've made it,' I whispered in Sue's single functioning aural orifice, in the hope that it still was. 'A naughty night-club at last!'

'How do you know it's naughty?' she asked.

I shrugged. 'Just a feeling,' I said. 'Three, to be precise.'

'What do you mean?'

'Three passes in five minutes. Not bad, is it? Very friendly, mind you, but fairly unequivocal. But then, I know I'm hard to resist. That's one of them over there,' I said, pointing to a dusky beauty who was dragging a bullet-headed young man onto the floor like a lamb to the slaughter. 'She nearly made me spill the drinks.'

'What did they say?' Sue asked.

'Nothing,' I replied. 'They just grabbed my cock.'

The music exploded again. 'FEELING FUNKY?' I bellowed, but it was no use, I had to revert to sign-language.

You couldn't call it dancing, it was more like a gang-bang, though nothing illegally indecent took place. Due to the congestion, buttock inevitably ground against buttock. Little puffs of hot breath popped in one's ear when one was least expecting it, and other people's sweat tickled down one's neck. Forewarned is forearmed, and on leaving the floor I kept a furtive hold of my manhood, as one might, in other circumstances, of one's wallet.

There was another merciful pause.

'I feel quite slighted,' Sue pouted. 'No one's made a pass at me.'

'People don't make passes at distinguished actresses,' I explained patiently, 'when the place is thick with whores.'

'You're dribbling your drink,' she riposted. 'I think it's time to go.'

*

A crippled boot-black pulled himself across the terrazzo on calloused knees, dumbly tapping on the toes of prospective customers to gain their attention. Through the indifferent throng of passengers, a wizened little gnome jostled his way brandishing a child's Flag of Cameroon, and shouting something unintelligible with irate self-importance.

On the runway, beyond the plate-glass windows and the variegated laurel hedge, our Boeing revved its engines to a roar. The little man pushed his way impatiently through the crowd, and stood facing his reflection in the glass, a look of passionate intensity kindling in his eyes. His chest swelling with pride, he slowly lifted his flag and, using it as a baton, he conducted the noise like Prospero commanding the tempest, every fibre of his being willing the engines on to an even greater crescendo of sound. The 'plane slowly turned on its axis, and infinitely slowly too, with the outstretched arms of a powerful magician, the old man turned and pointed imperiously in the direction in which the 'plane was already moving, which indoors just happened to be towards the gentlemen's toilet. As it taxied out of sight, he dropped his flag with a histrionic slump of the shoulders, and, after closely examining his watch, he nodded wisely to himself and shuffled off again, evidently unconcerned that no one gave him any credit for having controlled the whole tricky operation to perfection.

The Bight of Biafra dropped through a hole in the clouds and our African adventure was at an end. Four rumbustious children played 'tag' in the gangway all the way to Paris, and a terrified cat loosed its bowels over its owner's lap. British Airways would never allow such a thing. We had two hours to wait in the Station in Space which is called Charles de Gaulle Airport, and we decided to blow our last traveller's cheques on a dinner for two.

We whizzed like moon-walkers along the moving pavements, covering five yards with each weightless stride, then were sucked up through plastic tubes, while on the opposite side of the glass well others descended diagonally. We sat on white chairs at a white table on an ice-white mirrored floor with our hand-luggage, a little battered and bulging at the seams between our feet.

'Read me your diary,' I said. 'From the beginning.'

Sue scrabbled in her shoulder-bag and produced a little bound book.

'You realise it's not Tolstoy.' Like my own, it was telegrammatic and took only a short while to read.

'Your turn,' she said, and I obliged.

'What amazes me are the differences – the things you remember that I don't, and vice versa.'

'Do you think they would make a book?' I asked.

'I shouldn't think so,' she said.

'I thought of beginning with something like "On this trip, the acting profession seemed neither frivolous nor narcissistic, and the experience has immeasurably enriched our lives." '

'That's a bit pompous.'

'But it's true.'

She nodded pensively.

'You could try.'

'How about "Porter of Paddington is a pretty pompous name for a cat, but mine is a pompous cat...er...Yes. He clearly has aspirations to the Throne of Scotland, for every time I sat on it

I felt this 'orrible fat warm lump squirming beneath me complaining bitterly at being deposed…"?'

'That's worse.'

'P'raps I won't bother.'

She laughed, and looked at me for a long time as if at a stranger, though her eyes twinkled. Then she said, 'Love you.'

'Love you too,' I said.